D o'Driscøll

Queen's U. Bkstore ($80.88!!)
1/93

Growing up and going to school in Japan

Growing up and going to school in Japan

Tradition and Trends

Cyril Simmons

Open University Press
Milton Keynes · Philadelphia

Open University Press
Celtic Court
22 Ballmoor
Buckingham
MK18 1XW

and
1900 Frost Road, Suite 101
Bristol, PA 19007, USA

First Published 1990

British Library Cataloguing in Publication Data

Simmons, Cyril
    Growing up and going to school in Japan: traditions and trends.
    1. Japan. Education
    370'.952

    ISBN 0–335–09539–9

Library of Congress Cataloging-in-Publication Data

Simmons, Cyril, 1937–
    Growing up and going to school in Japan : tradition and trends /
Cyril Simmons.
        p.   cm.
    Includes bibliographical references.
    ISBN 0–335–09539–9
    1. Education–Japan–History.   2. Education–Japan–Aims and
objectives.   3. Youth–Japan–Conduct of life.   4. Comparative
education.   I. Title.
LA1311.S57   1990
370'.952—dc20   89–48154   CIP

Typeset by Colset Private Limited, Singapore
Printed and bound in Great Britain by
Woolnough Bookbinding Ltd, Irthlingborough, Northamptonshire

For my mother Naomi
and in memory of my father
Charles Harvey Simmons (1900–1988)

Contents

Preface

The purpose of this book is to present an up-to-date picture of schools in Japan together with a portrait of the young people who attend them. One simple reason for doing this is that, according to international tests of academic achievement, Japanese children are always among the best and frequently *are* the best in the world. This information is no longer of interest only to scholars but forms the basis of headlines in the popular press, for example, 'Land of the Rising Sons', which appeared in the *Daily Mail*, on 19 June 1989. This article, with its banner headlines and pictures of hundreds of hardworking school children, distils the essence of contemporary Japanese education as well as its significance. It is true, for example, that Britain 'is losing out against other countries in the education race', especially so when Britain is compared with Japan. It is equally true that Japanese companies are moving into Britain in increasing numbers and that, after a decade of high unemployment, British people are only too happy to work for them and, if need be, wear the company uniform and even sing the company song. So the question naturally arises as to what kind of education can produce in Japan the best-qualified workforce in the world.

At one level the answer seems to be simply that Japanese children work extremely hard at school. Indeed, most experience 'double schooling' since they also attend *juku* or cram school outside regular school hours. Also, most Japanese young people stay at school until they are aged 18 and *over half* remain in some form of full-time education beyond that age. At school most children behave impeccably. They respect their teachers, who are very well paid, and they respect the simple austere buildings in which they work—indeed, they clean their classrooms every day before going home. In addition, Japanese children are inured to what we in England and Wales are asked to accept as radical measures in the Education Reform Act of

1988. For example, a national curriculum has existed in Japan for decades and regular assessment is part of the air that Japanese children breathe. In fact, assessment rises to such a climax at 14 to secure entry into high school and at 17 to obtain university entrance that it has become known as *juken jigoku* or examination hell. Ironically, though, the more Western nations focus on Japan in the 1980s to learn something from their educational successes the more they discover that the Japanese themselves are seeking to change their highly competitive educational system into a more creative and less divisive one that will improve the quality of people's lives from the cradle to the grave.

An additional purpose of this book is to discover how the present educational system came into being and what it is that sustains Japanese children as they fight their way through *juken senso* or the examination war to the university or college of their choice. Chapters 1 and 2 are historical. The first surveys the Tokugawa era, famous for its *samurai* warriors, and compares the classical education of the military elite with the vocational training of the common people; while the second looks at the Meiji period, which saw a crash programme of modernization, industrialization and Westernization and which witnessed the prescient decision to introduce universal and compulsory elementary education for both *samurai* and people together. Chapter 3 looks at the origins of the present system of comprehensive education in the aftermath of the Pacific War and examines the phenomenon of 'double schooling' as well as the rise of the elite private schools. Chapter 4 seeks to understand something of the unique psychology of childhood and adolescence in Japan and its contribution to educational achievement while Chapter 5 describes and compares three major periods of educational reform in Britain and Japan, including that of the late 1980s.

All Japanese children from the age of six spend nine years in compulsory education (grades 1–9) and over 90 per cent continue for three more years at upper secondary or high school (grades 10–12). In Britain, by contrast, children begin an 11-year period of compulsory education at the age of five but only 33 per cent of 17-year-olds were still receiving full-time education in 1988 (DES 1988). The introduction of the National Curriculum in England and Wales in September 1989 provided for the first time an opportunity to introduce a uniform description of the school years but it is out of step with the Japanese system and many others. Therefore British year 2 equals Japanese grade 1 and so on.

In contemporary Japan writers addressing a Western audience usually follow Western custom in placing their given or forename before their family or surname. In this book, therefore, the names of Japanese figures and authors in the modern period are reported according to Western practice but in historical chapters the Japanese custom is followed — for it would be as odd to write Ieyasu Tokugawa as it would be to print Tudor Henry.

It is hoped that this book will be of interest to all who are fascinated by the phoenix-like rise of Japan in the post-war era, particularly in the field of education. It is, however, no more than an introduction and I am conscious that it will not escape the fate of all those volumes that presume to evaluate the Japanese experience. As Robert Smith (1983, p. 5) observed in the introduction to his four lectures on *Japanese Society*:

> Those who comment favourably on the achievements of Japanese society are accused of failing to pay sufficient attention to the high price paid for them; observers who stress their formidable personal and social costs are derided for their blindness to the positive social gains that have been made.

Acknowledgements

Few books can be written without assistance and this is certainly not one. First and foremost, I must thank Professor Saburo Iwawaki of Hyogo Graduate School of Education for making possible the Japanese part of the comparative study of young people's attitudes which is reported in Chapter 4 and out of which this larger project grew. It was Professor Iwawaki, too, who so generously gave of his time to introduce my wife and me to the fascinating cultural and religious centres of Ise, Nara and Kyoto. Thanks are also due to Tatsuya and Midori Todoroki for welcoming us to their home in Tokyo and to Midori especially for introducing us to the mysteries of the Metro and Shinkansen and helping us to keep our many appointments. My special thanks go to Lucy and Shinya Todoroki for translating the Japanese responses to my questionnaire into good modern English and for discussing many aspects of the life and education of young people in Japan. Thanks also to Maurice Jenkin of the British Council in Tokyo for arranging our schedule, to Yoshihito Yasuhara of the National Institute for Educational Research for translating my original paper into Japanese and to Professors Hiroshi Azuma and Tadahiko Inagaki of Tokyo University and Keiko Kashiwagi of Tokyo Women's University for being so generous with their time in discussing my research. In England, my thanks are due to several colleagues for reading parts of this book but in particular to Professor Cantor of Loughborough University for diligently reading the whole and making many well-informed comments. Thanks also go to Winnie Wade of Trent Polytechnic for doing so much early work on the statistics arising from both the English and the Japanese surveys and to the National Foundation for Educational Research for permission to rework material that originally appeared in their journal *Educational Research*. Any faults that remain after so much good advice must surely be mine and mine alone.

Finally, to the person who sustained me in so many ways throughout the long hours of writing and who transformed my much corrected longhand into excellent word-processed copy, my wife Chris, go the most heartfelt thanks of all.

Cyril Simmons
Loughborough

1

Education from Tokugawa to Meiji, 1600–1867

In 1598, Tokugawa Ieyasu, who came from a distinguished shogunate household, became a member of the council of guardians entrusted with the care of one Hideyori, the five-year-old son of Hideyoshi, the 'Napoleon of Japan', who had just died. This trust, in the case of Ieyasu, could not have been more completely misplaced, for in 1603 he established himself as *shogun* (or military leader) and set about ridding himself of Hideyori and his supporters. Then, in 1605, Ieyasu, who considered himself to be above all else a patient political operator, abdicated in favour of his son, though he continued to direct operations from his position behind the throne. In the event, he had to wait until the year of his own death in 1616 before Hideyori was finally driven to suicide and his supporters crushed. But the memorial to Ieyasu's patience was impressive: a succession of rulers that carried his family name forward for no less than 250 years. Quite remarkably, the Tokugawa Shogunate brought internal peace and isolation to Japan for two-and-a-half centuries. However, it also brought into being, through a network of agents, spies and checkpoints, a model police state.

In the nineteenth century, the West forced its attention on Japan. The Russians sought convenient ports where they could obtain supplies for eastern Siberia and Alaska. The British, at the height of aggressive Victorian capitalist expansion, wished to penetrate a market that remained defiantly closed to them. But it was the Americans, with their dream of becoming commercial leaders in China and Japan, who demanded and finally obtained a trade treaty in 1854. Treaties with Russia, Great Britain and France followed and the shogunate was perceived, quite rightly, as being unable to resist pressures from foreign powers. The shogunate thus became the natural target for criticism, and the throne, which had been shielded for centuries from the harsh realities of administrative power, became the natural symbol for nationalism.

In 1867, the 15-year-old Mutsuhito became emperor and adopted the title 'Meiji' which meant, appropriately enough, 'enlightened government'. Within a year, but after several months of civil war, the last Tokugawa *shogun*, Keiki, surrendered his administrative powers to the young emperor, the Meiji restoration was accomplished and a vast programme of modernization and Westernization was begun.

The purpose of this chapter is to describe the development of education during the Tokugawa period; but first it is necessary to explain something of what came before.

Chinese influences in Japan

At the beginning of the Tokugawa period 'the Chinese language was the royal road and the only road to all knowledge' (Dore, 1965, p. 136). This dominance of a foreign language in seventeenth-century Japan requires some explanation. Japan comprises four large islands and hundreds of smaller ones which lie in an arc off the coast of Asia. They are separated from the mainland by 100 miles of stormy sea. The Korea Strait, being four times wider than the Strait of Dover, was sufficient in ancient times to prevent any military invasion of the sort carried out by Julius Caesar in Britain. However, at about the same time as the Romans set foot on English soil (55 BC) a cultural invasion of Japan was beginning. Spearheaded by merchants and traders rather than by armies of soldiers, the invaders crossed the Korea Strait with artefacts and ideas from a Chinese civilization that had reached new heights under the Sing and Hang dynasties. This trading link was considerably strengthened in the fourth century AD when a Japanese colony was established on the tip of the Korean peninsula during the reign of the Empress Jingu. Communities of Korean and Chinese craftsmen followed the traders and brought artistic and technical skills with them that were superior to those of their adopted country. They also brought a religion and a script that are both much in evidence in Japan today: Buddhism provided a philosophy and a theology which the rather free-and-easy national religion of Shintoism lacked, and the Chinese language provided a form of writing to the letterless Japanese which ensured that the conquering culture would be enshrined in its own ideographs. To this day it is evident that the Japanese script is closely related to the Chinese, although the spoken languages differ very greatly. Bringing the two together must have involved considerable technical difficulties and for this reason alone it is likely that for many years the new form of writing was little known outside a small circle of scribes in the ruling imperial house.

By the seventh century AD Sinonization was proceeding apace. Crown Prince Shotoku, who was regent from 593 to 622, sat at the feet of visiting scholars in the Chinese classics and tradition credits him with becoming something of a scholar himself. He certainly encouraged young men at the court to study and sent students and priests to China. When they finally returned — and one scholar, Minabuchi Shoan, was away for 32 years — they were to be highly influential in advising Fujiwara Kamatari, a giant figure in Japanese history and another sinophile, to set up a reforming central government that would be the mirror image of China under the T'ang dynasty. Indeed, the new capital for the imperial court at Nara was a reconstruction of Ch'ang-an, the Chinese capital, and contains to this day some fine temples in the T'ang style of architecture. (Later, in 794, the capital city was moved to Kyoto and a second and even grander attempt was made to emulate Ch'ang-an.)

The Education Code (part of the Taiho Code of 701) was also Chinese in principle and laid down the first ever plan for a state system of education in Japan. It comprised a grand central school and provincial schools where potential young bureaucrats were to worship Confucius and study his doctrines on government and morals. In theory, the new system was to be a meritocracy in which able youths would pass examinations at 16 and be recommended for government posts, but in practice the schools were open only to the sons of influential parents whose boys were in any case frequently given exemption from examinations. Since the court aristocrats insisted on having government posts as of right there was, to say the least, little opportunity for social change through education in this early period. Doubtless a few ambitious youths achieved social mobility through the new schools but in general the social order remained unchanged and it was many centuries before a Japanese government would again initiate a national system of education for the good of the state.

It has often been observed that in Japanese history an era of consolidation follows a period of contact with a foreign civilization in which the borrowed culture is 'japanized' (Storry, 1976, p. 31). So it was with the Chinese 'invasion'. After some three centuries of thoroughgoing assimilation of all things Chinese a lengthy period of accommodation followed under the Fujiwara family in what is known as the Heian period (794–1185). For example, by the tenth century a system of abbreviated Chinese ideographs (*kana*), which represented phonetically the Japanese language, had been developed and had greatly assisted the flowering of indigenous literature. It seems that women writers in particular used the new syllabary possibly because it caught so accurately the sound of spoken Japanese. Male writers seemed to prefer Chinese and until modern times scholarly prestige still attached to writing Chinese in the classical form.

Most of the artistic and cultural endeavour of this period arose from the aristocrats who lived a life of exquisite formality at court in Kyoto. The central government posts described in the Taiho code, traditionally occupied by the heads of great families, became increasingly ritualistic and removed from their original purpose. Thus life at court was devoted to the development of aesthetic values with the corollary that the day-to-day government of the country drifted away from the centre to the estate and household offices of the leading families. Thus, during the Heian period, there developed at Kyoto a profound love of learning and a delight in artistic achievement that was to remain with the Japanese people for ever. But away from the capital ordinary people took note only of the growing powers of ambitious local chieftains, privileged Buddhist monks and agents of the Fujiwaras to whom they paid taxes in an increasingly feudal manner.

Education also changed. The grand school increasingly attracted only the sons of aristocrats and when it became obvious that the government posts for which these young people were being prepared were largely nominal, education fell into decline. Government support for the central school dried up and when the school was destroyed by fire in 1177 no attempt was made to rebuild it. Provincial schools fared little better. Few were ever actually built and of those that were one of the best in northern Kyushu had disappeared from the records by the tenth century. However, the decline of the state system of education led to the foundation of a number of private schools. These arose in boarding houses that had been built by the landed gentry for their sons who were up from the provinces to attend the central school. The estates of the leading families needed educated administrators and so up to five private schools were founded between the eighth and thirteenth centuries for this purpose.

The Heian period, then, saw considerable change in education, the arts and government. To ordinary people, though, the greatest of these must have been the last. Buddhist monks grew more wealthy and worldly on their tax-free estates and became so sensitive about security that they raised military units in order to protect their lands. Similarly, local chieftains and provincial Fujiwaras flexed their muscles. They also enjoyed tax-free estates and developed a taste for military might. The court aristocrats at first found it useful to call in military aid from the chieftains to sort out brawls in the capital between competing bands of Buddhist and Confucian supporters, but inevitably, or so it seems with hindsight, the clans were called in to sort out quarrels between elements within the vast Fujiwara family itself. Finally, of course, the tables were turned and the aristocrats discovered that they were the servants and not the masters of the new military houses that had evolved. Military government had arrived in Japan and was to last under six successive families from the twelfth to the nineteenth century.

Appropriately enough, military power was inaugurated with murder, intrigue and suicide as the Fujiwara were overthrown by the Taira who were in turn defeated by the Minamoto at a historic sea battle in 1185. In the hands of writers and poets, a wonderfully romantic view of this age

developed in which chivalrous *samurai* warriors with impassive faces
and colourful armour rode through forests of bamboo and pine. Somewhat less romantic was the new and particularly nasty form of suicide,
the *hara-kiri*, that was also a product of this period.

Military power was consolidated in a number of ways. A new capital, Kamakura, was established south of modern Tokyo and at a considerable distance from the artistic and cultural life at Kyoto. At
Kamakura a new style of national administration — the *Bakufu* or
camp office — was set up which soon proved itself more effective than
that of the imperial government. Finally, Minamoto Yoritomo was
confirmed by the emperor in the title of *shogun*, which henceforth
became synonymous with a permanent rather than a temporary military position.

The Kamakura *Bakufu* survived external threat in 1281 in the form
of a massive Mongol armada, through the intervention of a typhoon
that was subsequently renamed the 'Divine Wind' or *kamikaze*, but it
succumbed to internal threat in 1333 when Kamakura itself fell to
supporters of the Emperor Daigo. However, after a short time power
returned to the house of Minamoto in the person of Ashikaga Takauji.
He had himself appointed *shogun* and set up his government in the
Muromachi district of Kyoto, where it remained until 1573. Once
again there was a great flourishing of the arts at Kyoto and the *shogun*
lived in shameless luxury while the imperial court in the same city
was reduced to penury. Outside Kyoto conditions were chaotic and the
fortunes of the great families, in the absence of law and order, were
settled according to the laws of the jungle. At the same time, despite
the turmoil, the economy developed, trade with China was renewed
and the education of young warriors was undertaken.

The education of warriors before Tokugawa was practical rather
than literary. The educational ideal during the early period of military
government certainly included proficiency in both academic and military arts but in fact there were few warrior scholars and illiteracy
was widespread. According to the chronicle of Nitta Yoshisada
(1301–1338):

> From ancient times until the present day, military arms and the pen
> have been considered as two virtues like heaven and earth. Lacking
> one of them, one cannot control the affairs of a state. Therefore, the
> nobles primarily engage in literature and learn such arts as poetry-
> making and music. But for statesmen arms are of the utmost impor-
> tance. These consist of archery, horsemanship and strategy (quoted
> in Kaigo, 1968, p. 19).

The last-named skills were taught by example in the home and on the
battlefield and, according to one record from the Kamakura period,
from a child's early years:

As he became five or six years old, I taught him to take a small bow and arrows of small bamboo and to shoot at targets, deer targets, rabbits and to ride on horseback after rabbits and deer (quoted in Kaigo, 1968, p. 21).

The warrior children practised every day on archery ranges and riding areas and frequently witnessed their elders combine both skills in competitions where the goal was to shoot at targets from horseback. Training in swordsmanship was also an important part of the young warrior's curriculum. Some also learned the 48 techniques of the new art of *sumo* or wrestling.

There was only one true educational test for aspiring warriors, and that was the battlefield. There the honour of families could be enhanced or damaged for evermore. Fathers actively sought out opportunities for their sons to learn the arts of war in actual combat but when periods of peace intervened the grand hunt provided a satisfactory substitute. It was universally recognized that to catch game demanded bravery and to take deer and wild boar resulted in honours equal to those awarded for killing an enemy general.

We have seen that the first attempt to found a state system of education had collapsed by the twelfth century, although a few private schools were founded in redundant boarding houses. That any form of institutionalized education was kept alive during the Kamakura period was due entirely to the Buddhist temples. The temples had always offered a form of education to would-be priests since the novices needed to be trained in order to read the *sutras*, but from the twelfth century onwards this education was enlarged somewhat. It was broadened academically to include secular studies which could be pursued by the most able students to very high levels and it was broadened socially to include lay children who could obtain an elementary education of up to five years' duration. Furthermore, because of Buddhist egalitarianism there was some mixing of the social classes and, by the fifteenth century, it was not uncommon for sons of wealthy commoners to sit alongside the sons of the *samurai* in the temple schools reading the *sutras* and practising penmanship.

The form of Buddhism that appealed most particularly to warriors, aristocrats and scholars was Zen. Zen was not a 'popular' sect because it lacked ritual and sacred texts and called for discipline and meditation, but it offered enlightenment and supported the *samurai* ideals of fidelity and indifference to physical hardship. Zen was also Chinese in origin. So at the same time as trade contacts were being renewed with China after an interval of several centuries, scholarly output was also on the increase in the study of Chinese literature among the priests at the Zen Buddhist temples. However, it is important to keep these developments in perspective. The warriors or *samurai*, from the *shogun* and *daimyos* (feudal lords) down to the humble foot-soldiers, made up only a very small part of the population and, according to one Japanese writer, any able-bodied priest worth his salt would seek honour on the battlefield rather than distinction in the temple.

> Those priests who were of a bold and robust disposition got themselves a lance and set out for the battlefield. Hence, the only people concerned with letters were a few weakly priests, a few weakly Confucian scholars, doctors, calligraphers and painters (quoted in Dore, 1965, p. 1).

This anonymous writer, from the vantage point of the seventeenth century, describes the political confusion of the hundred years or so leading up to the rise of Tokugawa Ieyasu and concludes that education came a very poor second to war. Interestingly, it was into this confusion that the first Europeans arrived in Japan in about 1542 bringing with them an organ of education — Christianity — and an instrument of war — the smooth bore musket. In the event it was the musket that was more highly valued and which secured peace for two-and-a-half centuries. Craftsmen quickly learned not only how to make the musket but also how to decorate and improve the weapon so that the art of the gunsmith, like that of the swordsmith in earlier centuries, was raised to new levels of skill and beauty. More to the point, Oda Nobunaga, a powerful and ambitious *daimyo*, saw the practical possibilities offered by the new weapon. He became the first feudal lord to equip a major part of his army with muskets and, after a series of military victories, emerged as the foremost figure in the land. His rise to power was greatly assisted by his vassal, Hideyoshi, and his devoted ally, Tokugawa Ieyasu, the very same Ieyasu with whom this chapter began. It was he who was entrusted with the care of Hideyoshi's five-year-old son but who determined instead that his own son, Hidetada, should be *shogun*. As we have seen, Ieyasu was entirely successful in his ambition and became the first of fifteen *shogun* to bear the family name of Tokugawa. The last, Keiki, died in the twentieth century.

The Tokugawa were united in a common desire to preserve a static and hierarchical society. To this end, they policed the state with zeal, and particularly the *Tokaido* — the principal highway between Kyoto and Edo (modern Tokyo and seat of the Tokugawa Shogunate). The main travellers on this road were the western *daimyo* who were required to spend part of every year at Edo engaging in ritual and ceremony under the eye of the shogun. On their return to the provinces they were obliged to leave their wives and children in Edo as hostages in all but name. In addition, and for our present purposes most importantly, the Tokugawa from Ieyasu onwards encouraged the study of the Chinese classics, for Confucianism, with its emphasis on the duties of inferiors to superiors and the supreme importance of harmony within the state, was seen as an ideology that would secure the hearts and minds of the people as effectively as spies and agents secured the *Tokaido*.

Education during the Tokugawa period (1600–1867)

> The arts of peace and war, including archery and horsemanship, should be pursued single-mindedly. From of old the rule has been to practice 'the arts of peace on the left hand and the arts of war on the right'.

These words are usually attributed to Tokugawa Ieyasu and are found in 'Laws Governing the Military Households', a collection of exhortations to the military classes which was issued in 1615 (Passin, 1965, p. 163). It is noteworthy that Ieyasu's order of priorities differs from those chronicled by Nitta Yoshisada in the earlier military periods (see Kaigo, 1968, p. 19). Nitta gave military arts precedence over the pen, whereas in Ieyasu's maxim the arts of peace (*bun*) preceded the arts of war (*bu*). Later *shogun* followed him in this new emphasis and so there came about a considerable transformation in the education of the *samurai*. Socially, however, there was little change.

Tokugawa society was a warrior society and the *samurai* were supreme. They lived in magnificent houses and mansions and were literally a class apart from the commoners — farmers, artisans and merchants. (The nobility at this time were few in number and had little influence.) The *samurai*, however, were now warriors only in name. Military skills still had their place in Tokugawa society but they could no longer be exercised on the battlefield. Consequently they came to be valued less than in former times. The warriors continued to guard jealously their privilege of wearing two swords but these symbols of the arts of war gave way, in obedience to the *shogun*'s injunction, to symbols of the arts of peace. In short, the *samurai* wanted schools for their children and wished to give them an education that set them apart from ordinary men — they gave little thought to the education of women. Thus the schools and the education they offered became over time symbols of a new class of wealthy bureaucrats and administrators who had left the battlefield and the chase for books and the pen.

The education of the samurai

The chief aims of *samurai* education, drawn from Confucian tradition, were moral rather than intellectual, spiritual rather than utilitarian. Education was seen as a personal pilgrimage that would produce benefits for the state. The first duty of man was to choose a life of virtue. Virtue could be exercised in five main areas of human interaction. Thus between parents and children, master and servant, husband and wife, younger and elder siblings and friends, there could be love, loyalty, respect, human kindness and trust as appropriate to each relationship. The belief that the chief end of study is virtue led, ineluctably, to the affirmation that those who had studied well would also govern well. Thus the second duty of man was to strive for the common weal. These twin aims of education were epitomized in the opening statement of principles of the Hikone fief school for *samurai* and were read every month to the students:

> The essentials of book learning (*bun*) are, cultivating as a basis the 'way' of filial piety, respect for elders, loyalty and trust, to clarify the principles whereby nations are governed and the people made content, and so to strive to be useful in the public service (Dore, 1965, p. 43).

However, as the eighteenth century wore on a new word entered the vocabulary of educational policy. The need for identifying talent (*jinzai*) among the *samurai* became ever more pressing. The *Bakufu*, or national administration first set up at Kamakura, was faced with increasingly complex management problems and needed to recruit the most gifted of the *samurai* to sort them out. There was no suggestion at this stage that able administrators outside the ranks of the warriors might be recruited to top jobs. The question naturally arose whether being well versed in Chinese classics and being taught by Chinese scholars without experience of government was in any way a suitable preparation for the life of a mandarin. However, there seemed to be no answer to this question since the scholars, with their reverence for the Chinese past, and the *samurai*, with their distaste for the practical present, both prevented serious educational reforms from taking place until Western learning burst upon the scene in the nineteenth century.

There had, however, been intimations of Western learning in Japan from the very beginning of the period. In 1600, while Tokugawa Ieyasu had been exercising his guardianship of the young Hideyori with all the outward appearance of benevolence, a Dutch ship limped into port with less than a quarter of her original crew alive. One of the survivors was the pilot, Will Adams, who was the first Englishman to set foot on Japanese soil. He got on extremely well with Ieyasu and taught him mathematics and navigation as well as informing him of European affairs. However, it was not until 1740 that *Shogun* Yoshimune officially approved the study of certain technical subjects outside the competence of Confucian scholars such as medicine, cartography and technology, and it was only at the very end of the period that academies were set up to teach Western military practice (the Kobusho in 1856) and Western science and languages (the Kaiseijo in 1863).

From the early days of the Tokugawa era there were three main types of school for *samurai* boys. These were provided by the government (*Bakufu*), the fiefs or domains (*han*) and private individuals (*shijuku*). Government-sponsored education began with a subsidy in 1630 to build the Shoheiko in Edo — sometimes called the Hayashi school after the family that founded it. The *Bakufu* financed a splendid rebuilding programme of the Shoheiko in the 1690s and eventually in the eighteenth century assumed full control of the school, appointing staff and laying down the curriculum. The Shoheiko became highly influential. It was the centre for the teaching of Confucian orthodoxy (the Chu Hsi doctrine) which from 1790 became the *only* permitted form of Confucianism. There was therefore little academic freedom in Tokugawa Japan since *Bakufu* schools were in the business of producing orthodox citizens rather than seekers after truth. In all, the government controlled directly over 20 schools, some of the most important of which were founded towards the end of the period. These last specialized in subjects such as oriental and occidental medicine, Japanese and occidental literature and military science. Some survived into the modern era and became forerunners of university colleges in Edo.

The *han* or fief schools greatly outnumbered *Bakufu* schools by the end of the period. Altogether there were some 250 fiefs but because the *daimyos* who held these could be transferred from one fief to another or even disfeoffed by the *shogun* the number was never constant. By the end of the era there were schools in over 200 domains, but at the beginning progress was slow with only 15 fiefs founding schools in the seventeenth century. Fiefs held by *daimyos* who were themselves scholars were among the first to have schools but in the eighteenth and nineteenth centuries progress was much more rapid because the lead taken by the *Bakufu* in funding the Shoheiko acted as a considerable spur to less scholarly *daimyos*. Doubtless fashion, too, played its part when it became evident that fief schools were the order of the day. Government control was maintained in *han* schools because *daimyos* could not afford to sponsor other than orthodox doctrines and because many of the teachers were graduates of the Shoheiko. However, there was little uniformity in the size and location of *han* schools. The larger clans possessed fine schools with imposing buildings close to the *daimyos'* castles but elsewhere smaller provincial schools (*gogaku*) were built in towns. Sometimes it was possible for commoners to attend lectures at the *gogaku* and in the very last years of the Shogunate increasing numbers of commoners were educated alongside the *samurai*.

The *shijuku* or private schools also lacked uniformity. They differed in the degree to which they received support from the fief, indeed many received no support at all. They differed in their curricula and for that reason were less open to control than the *Bakufu* or *han* schools.

Many, of course, provided Confucian and Japanese studies but some offered Western languages, Dutch studies, medicine, mathematics and navigation. Some attracted students nationwide on account of their teachers, who were famous for their political, philosophical or educational views, while others quietly served the local community. Some, indeed most, attracted largely *samurai* students while a few and particularly one in Kyoto (Ito Jinsai's Kogido) attracted many commoners. Some were tiny schools with 20 or so students whereas others were vast academies catering for thousands. Altogether there were about 1,500 private schools at the end of the period.

The role of the *shijuku* in introducing new areas of learning and encouraging students to question orthodox views is important in understanding the final years of the Tokugawa period. Thus, one romantic and idealistic teacher, Yoshida Shoin, attracted and inspired many *samurai* who later played a key part in the Meiji restoration. Shoin revered the Chinese classics but saw the need for the pursuit of learning to break out of the straitjacket of isolation imposed on it by the shogunate, and for it 'to be fully acquainted with conditions all over the world' (Passin, 1965, p. 203). This need was seen most keenly by the young Emperor Meiji who stated it formally in his 'Charter Oath' in 1868, nine years after the death of Shoin.

However, the traditional curriculum as experienced by most *samurai* acquainted them with the Chinese past only. It comprised calligraphy, the Chinese classics and a little arithmetic, with some practice in etiquette and the military arts. One feature of this education which at first sight seems difficult to believe is that the warriors were taught to *write* in Japanese but to *read* in Chinese. This odd state of affairs came about because although the Japanese had adopted the Chinese form of writing and had, over many generations, transformed it into a Japanese script, they continued to venerate the Chinese classics, which had never been translated into the vernacular, and to read them only in Chinese. The two scripts were, of course, closely related but this was not always obvious since Japanese was printed and written in cursive script whereas Chinese was printed and usually written in square characters. Many characters were shared by both scripts but understandably many characters in the Chinese classics had no counterpart in contemporary Japanese writing. So although Japanese had become an accepted form of official communication and basic Japanese literacy had become the aim of many of the non-*samurai*, reading the classics in Chinese remained the only path to wisdom and therefore the most important part of *samurai* education.

The *samurai* learnt first to write, but such was the low status of calligraphy that it might not be included in the curriculum of the fief school and tuition would have to be sought privately. When tuition was found calligraphy would be taught almost exclusively by copying,

with endless repetition, from models and since calligraphy was considered an art form as much as a skill it had to be approached with all due
seriousness and concentration. The goal was perfection and the only
acceptable norm was a good script.

The young warriors having obtained a grounding in calligraphy by
the age of seven or eight would make their first acquaintance with the
classics. A favourite first reader was the 'Classic of Filial Piety' by
reason of its appropriate moral tone. Repetition (or *sodoku*) was again
the prescribed method by which the classics were mastered. Perhaps
there was no other way, for the task confronting the *samurai* was
difficult in the extreme. The Chinese text had to be 'read off' in Japanese rather than read in Chinese by means of an elaborate system of
notation which had taken centuries to devise. This allowed young
students to render Chinese in a strange and formal Japanese quite
unlike their everyday use of the language. Progress was painfully slow.
At the beginning, a handful of characters would be attempted every
day. The child would go through the phrase with the teacher until he
could repeat it by himself and then would read it over and over again
throughout the morning. Later in his schooling he would attempt
several phrases or even half a page every morning. By these means the
Four Books (*Analects*, *Mencius*, *Greater Learning*, *Golden Mean*) and
possibly the Five Classics as well were learnt by rote by the age of 13 or
14. For many teachers *sodoku* was an end in itself, but for the more
scholarly analysis and exegesis of the text was also important. The
latter probably inspired young *samurai* with a sense of the literature
they were reading while the former produced alumni with only a limited understanding of the Chinese language or its classic texts. *Sodoku*
itself, however, became deeply embedded in the Japanese psyche as a
powerful means of learning difficult educational material.

Brighter children, after *sodoku*, passed on to higher things. Detailed
commentaries were available to facilitate further study of the classics.
Alternatively, a whole range of books was available, all Chinese, on
history, literature, medicine, astronomy, mathematics and law.
Samurai would read up to ten pages a day and mark difficult passages
for individual discussion with the teacher. Group reading (*kaidoku*)
and group discussion (*rinko*) were also popular. Some teachers, however, preferred to lecture. This mode of teaching increased in popularity towards the end of the seventeenth century after *Shogun*
Tsunayoshi showed considerable interest in both attending and deliv-
ering lectures himself.

Most schools possessed lecture rooms, indeed in many cases the
lecture hall was the first part of the school to be built. The lectures
themselves varied in style as well as popularity with the listeners.
Some lecturers examined the classics in minute detail in much the
same way as they discussed the text with individuals, whereas others

tended to sermonize on broader moral issues and introduce amusing anecdotes in order to maintain the interest of their audience. The former type of lecture seems to have been the more common, with *samurai* assiduously writing down every word uttered. However, both types of lecture had their critics. The first was castigated by Hayashi Shihei (of the Shoheiko school in Edo) as 'useless' because the student would 'end up with nothing in his head and an unintelligible jumble in his notebook' and the second was scorned by Ogyu Sorai (1666–1728), an outstanding scholar and critic, as 'a practice which degrades the teacher's character and corrupts the student's intellect' (Dore, 1967, p. 140). Probably the average lecture *was* pretty dry and was attended by the *samurai* more out of a sense of duty than out of any expectation that enlightenment would be forthcoming.

Finally, for those who had passed beyond *sodoku* and had gained from lectures and discussions, a written examination could be taken between the ages of 15 and 20. This amounted to a test, in Japanese, of the candidates' powers of elucidation of short passages from the classics. To what degree a good performance in a written examination was predictive of administrative competence was a matter for debate. However, since examinations became increasingly common as the period progressed it would appear that there was a growing acceptance of the notion that some relationship existed between the two. Nevertheless, more general records of achievement were kept by many schools so that excellence in examinations was never the sole arbiter for placing *samurai* in administrative posts. Certainly one important aspect of a warrior's education, in addition to his moral development, was his general ability to conduct himself appropriately in a feudal society. In the military arts, for example, training had become more a matter of formalized, ritualized and disciplined gymnastics than the sometimes bloody encounters that had been tolerated between rival schools of swordsmanship at the beginning of the period. More generally, the practice of etiquette and ceremonial became ever more exacting and no *samurai*'s education was complete until the complexities of good manners, particularly with regard to seating manners, had been mastered.

Dore (1965, p. 152) concludes that much *samurai* education was 'quite plainly dull and in addition almost meaningless' but that 'the formalism of the education they received helped to produce men capable of maintaining the niceties of rank and status on which the stability of the social order depended'.

The education of commoners

It was axiomatic in Tokugawa society that the *samurai* be educated, so the *Bakufu*, the *han* and the *shijuku* provided the means. By contrast, it was a matter for debate whether commoners should be educated at all outside the home and so provision from official sources was meagre in the extreme. Nevertheless at the end of the era about 50 per cent of young commoners were receiving a formal, elementary education — which, in the absence of significant financial support from the *Bakufu*, was a remarkable achievement.

It is true that a few high-ranking commoners of superior intelligence received an education at the *han* schools both at the beginning of the Tokugawa period, before the *samurai* had lost touch completely with their own peasant origins, and at the end when the need to discover people of talent was urgent. However, tolerance of commoners at the fief schools was enhanced if they were preparing themselves for a life of scholarship and was contingent on their accepting their place in society as second-class citizens. Indeed, at the *Bakufu* school, the Shoheiko, a condition of commoner entry after 1793 was that students be admitted to the lowest rank and give up their family trade. It is not really surprising that commoners were poorly represented in *han* and *Bakufu* schools since low-ranking *samurai* (e.g., foot-soldiers) were often excluded and even the higher ranks meticulously observed fine distinctions between themselves — such as how many retainers should accompany the student to school and how many servants should be allowed to mind their sandals and umbrellas. What *is* perhaps surprising is that scholarship was seen as such a harmless occupation for talented commoners.

Lower-rank commoners of less obvious talent than the prospective scholars had a hard time of it in Tokugawa Japan. Oscillating rice prices and oppressive levels of taxation, coupled with periods of famine, led to the practice of *mabiki* (infanticide). Appropriately enough for the commoners the word was taken directly from that for the task of 'thinning out' young rice plants. This practice shocked Haya Kawa Hachirozaemon, the intendant in the 1790s of the Okayama prefecture, and he determined to lecture the people on their wicked ways. He later employed two Confucian scholars to assist him in his task and encouraged the building of schools for adult moral education and child literacy. These schools and others like them seem to have been financed by wealthy local farmers with some assistance from the *Bakufu*. The strong moral purpose behind these initiatives is reminiscent of the Churches' missionary approach to elementary education in Britain. In fact a further parallel exists in so far as the Church societies in England eventually attracted government moneys to support their educational efforts (Wardle, 1970). In Tokugawa society moral instruction and exhortation from the authorities was a regular feature of everyday life. In towns and villages, for example, notice boards contained a mixture of secular and moral injunctions of the Confucian sort, as did the preface to the local census register. The latter was intended by the authorities to be read by the local headman to the assembled community. The moral sections were largely concerned with honouring parents and respecting superiors; to encourage the populace further, rewards in the shape of gifts or public recognition were made to those whose filial conduct appeared exceptional. Doubtless commoners listened to moral readings with polite patience and were suitably pleased when virtue was rewarded but what they increasingly desired as the period unfolded was to emulate the headman in his ability to read, write and understand something of the classics. To achieve these ends they turned in growing numbers to the *terakoya*.

Terakoya means literally 'children of the temple' and derives from the period between the twelfth and sixteenth centuries when, for lack of any other institution of formal education, lay children attended Buddhist temple schools. In the Tokugawa period, however, *terakoya* lost its religious connotation and came to mean simply a house which takes pupils. Sometimes the 'house' was in fact a shrine or temple but it might equally have been a requisitioned empty building or even the teacher's own home. Sometimes the new 'houses' or schools were set up on a charitable basis by priests, doctors, local officials or wealthy farmers. In this case the benefactors might teach in the schools themselves, employ a teacher or accept the services of a local dignitary or retired person. In other cases, particularly in the towns, some people who had difficulty in earning a living turned to teaching for a livelihood — although the rewards were never great. This new breed of teacher comprised dispossessed *samurai* (*Ronin*), widows and spinsters, and professionals who were prevented from following their usual calling by some physical disability. Overall one of the most interesting changes during the period was the nation-wide fall in the proportion of teachers who were priests from half to a quarter, and the rise in Edo in the proportion of teachers who were commoners from next to nothing to over half. This indicates both the secular nature of the *terakoya* and also the rising educational achievement of commoners, particularly in the urban areas.

The demand for popular education in the *terakoya* increased throughout the Tokugawa period but most rapidly during the nineteenth century. It is generally agreed, although the evidence is often fragmentary, that in 1850 there were over 6000 *terakoya*, but that this figure doubled by the end of the era (1867). Demand was greatest in the towns and cities, where it seems likely that the majority of boys received some form of elementary education outside the home. For the merchant class in particular, although regarded as the lowest of the social classes, the Tokugawa period became one of great prosperity. Hence the sons of merchants attended first the *terakoya* and then became apprentices in order to carry their education further. In the country, schools were less accessible and demand was less than in the urban areas; nevertheless, village leaders and heads of neighbourhood associations (a lower level in the administrative hierarchy of local government) wished to be literate and more besides. Village headmen frequently wished to emulate the lifestyles of the *samurai* and to this end they built up small libraries in order to broaden their knowledge and understanding of the classics.

Terakoya education arose in response to popular demand and was tailored to popular taste. It was unfettered by the *Bakufu* — largely because it attracted very little government attention for most of the period. The schools differed in size (on average between 30 and 60 students) and the instruction varied in quality but the curriculum, unlike that of the *samurai* schools, was practically and vocationally orientated and was open to girls as well as boys. Girls were outnumbered by boys and were rigidly segregated from them but they probably enjoyed, on average, an education of about five years compared to the boys' four. Attendance at school for both boys and girls was adjusted to their outside work requirements and, as in English schools of the same period, the long holiday was taken when the agricultural season was at its height.

Parallels with English schools, however, cannot usefully be carried much further. Whereas in Japan tuition for *samurai* and commoners alike included much personal instruction in reading and writing, the English 'monitorial' system and the 'simultaneous' system that followed it ensured that for much of the nineteenth century the children of English commoners received little in the way of individual tuition. Certainly in the seventeenth and eighteenth centuries elementary schools in Britain of between 20 and 40 pupils had allowed personal work and consultation with the teacher but the nineteenth century schools with up to 500 pupils supervised by one teacher and his band of monitors meant that pupils received very little personal attention. Similarly, the 'simultaneous' system in which one whole class received simultaneous instruction in one body of material meant that there was little allowance for individual differences in pupils. Thus although rote learning was common in both countries in the nineteenth century it is likely that individual tuition tailored to the needs of individual pupils was more common in Japan.

The staple diet in the curriculum of the *terakoya* was calligraphy. (The ability to read was thought to arise naturally through endless attention to writing.) The day would start with the pupil receiving personal instruction from the teacher and continue with many hours of writing practice following the morning's lesson. Pupils would use and reuse cheap note books until both they and the books were ebony black. Kaigo (1968, p. 42) quotes a contemporary report that 'Many children, with their faces, hands and legs stained with ink, look like negroes. With their eyes alone shining, they come in [the bath] with a lot of noise.' Many hundreds of textbooks were available to assist young commoners in learning to write and some of the most popular were several centuries old. The traditional method of teaching writing dated back to the Heian period and involved copying letters of the sort written by aristocrats to each other during the course of a year. This method meant that young nineteenth-century commoner copyists solemnly wrote for many hours each week about the passing of the seasons and everyday life in Japan in the Middle Ages. Few criticized this method of learning because it was time-honoured and hallowed by tradition, but it did lead to some curious anomolies. Individual words used in ancient texts were no longer current in the pupils' own time and some of the institutions described had ceased to exist. To overcome these difficulties, annotated and illustrated editions proliferated. Interestingly, some of the most delightful illustrations bore little relation to the accompanying text but provided instead a charming commentary on life during the Tokugawa period.

Moral education also had its place in the *terakoya*. Two ancient texts, *Jitsugokyo* and *Dojikyo*, were very popular and certain passages from these works entered the vocabulary of Tokugawa commoners in much the same way as phrases from Shakespeare and the Bible have permeated the English language. According to Kaigo (1968, p. 44), *Jitsugokyo* was used as a textbook for elementary education in Japan for over seven hundred years. The origin of these two texts was Chinese and the morality Confucian though filtered by Buddhist priests to make the essentially agnostic Chinese philosophy more acceptable to the common people. Characteristically, there was much emphasis on filial duties and respect for teachers. Indeed the *Jitsugokyo* contains the exhortation: 'Your father and your mother are like heaven and earth, your teacher and your lord are like the sun and the moon. All other relations may be likened to useless stones' (quoted in Dore, 1965, p. 276). Extreme expressions of this sort also accompany exhortations to study and may have been delivered by teachers at the end of the morning sessions when the class came together for moral instruction and chorus-type recitations of 'tables', local folktales and extracts from the more popular texts.

In addition to the general texts discussed above there were also more specific texts in the form of vocabularies for the children of merchants, farmers, sailors and many more occupational groups. Other texts provided geographical and historical information often laced with moral precepts and sycophantic praise for the shogunate's public works. Most of these books were intended for boys although a few were written specifically for girls. The latter reflect a society in which women's roles were closely defined. Girls' books contained, if anything, more moral instruction than the boys' but also much practical advice on pregnancy, childbirth, etiquette, cosmetics and female accomplishments. An important aim in books for both sexes was to describe appropriate behaviour along with suitable moral sanctions so that the status quo of Tokugawa society would be preserved.

The *terakoya*, then, excelled at writing practice, encouraged reading and offered simple pre-vocational education. The *terakoya* arose because of the aspirations of commoners, the public-spiritedness of many higher-ranking individuals and the early stirrings of educational entrepreneurial activity in Japan. They were not by and large of much interest to the *Bakufu*, despite the fact that throughout most of the period they provided the only elementary education that most commoners would experience outside the home apart from the formal apprenticeship system.

The merchant class, as we have noted, became increasingly successful and wealthy during the Tokugawa period. The *samurai* regarded the whole subject of commerce with some distaste and, by association, thought of arithmetic as a subject tainted by merchants and therefore not really suitable for their children. By contrast, the *terakoya*, in urban areas, introduced children to the abacus and simple arithmetical exercises as a matter of course. But for further training in mathematics and financial matters the sons of merchants would need to be apprenticed to a local business house. They would be articled at the age of 10 or so for about ten years according to a system that had been developed by the rising capitalist class. As with apprenticeship systems worldwide, young boys were occupied with menial tasks in the early years and·subjected to strict discipline. In Japan, however, in the evening their education would continue with studies in the three Rs. At the ages of 15 and 18 the boys would be given increased responsibilities and at about 20, when they attained their majority, they would be treated for the first time as members of the household in which they worked and they would be launched on their career.

The daughters of merchants also experienced a form of apprenticeship tailored to fit their perceived needs. At the age of 14 or 15 years they became maids in large households and discovered at first hand the realities of domestic management, on the one hand, and social skills, on the other. Their education in reading, writing, music and dancing also continued, although this is not mentioned in the following passage from a story cited by Kaigo (1968, p. 46) in which a merchant's wife expresses her approval of the socialization of daughters outside the family home:

Housemaid service is important. One learns good manners without being taught. So long as a girl lives with her parents, even the severest words cannot correct her bad manners. Once she is sent to a mansion of a lord, her manners gradually improve in one way or another.

It seems very likely that this passage reflects a more general belief among merchants, successful farmers and craftsmen that by placing their children away from home on educational apprenticeships they were encouraging their early development in independence and maturity. A contemporary proverb sums it all up: 'if you love your child send him on a journey' (see Dore, 1965, p. 268). Specifically, though, this passage may reflect the social ambitions of the merchant class, for if one's daughter became a maid in a *daimyo*'s mansion then she might marry into the lower reaches of the *samurai*. At first sight this might seem an unrealistic ambition since the four orders in Tokugawa society the *samurai* came first and the merchants last with the farmers and craftsmen intervening. But times were changing. At the beginning of the Tokugawa period rice was the principal means of exchange and the *samurai* received their income from *shogun* or *daimyo* in that cereal, but at the end of the era money was the means of exchange and the *samurai* came to the merchants to sell their rice in exchange for coin. Power relationships were also changing with a few merchants achieving *samurai* status through marriage or adoption and some *samurai* becoming merchants through necessity. It is significant that some of the most powerful merchant houses of the nineteenth century, for example, the house of Mitsui, are huge capitalist combines today.

Lacking status, despite their growing wealth, many merchants found comfort in the teachings of a great religious figure of the early eighteenth century, Ishida Baigan (1685–1744). He founded the *Shingaku* movement which, with its emphasis on people improving themselves by their own efforts, both appealed to merchants and also caused ripples of disapproval in the establishment. His unorthodoxy consisted not in his Confucianism but in his belief that by employing homely teaching methods it was possible to make comprehensible to commoners the life of virtue and the higher learning. By the end of the period *Shingaku* had spread from Kyoto to Edo and had gained considerable support from the commoners. Up to 200 schools were founded for children and, for adults, lecture halls were constructed in which crowded meetings took place. The establishment was mollified when it realized that *Shingaku*'s chief aim was to encourage the practice of virtue rather than insurrection and so it approved and patronized the movement and thus effectively nullified any revolutionary tendency it might have contained.

Conclusion

Any analysis of the considerable educational achievements of the Japanese in the present century is bound to be incomplete without some understanding of the historical and cultural context in which these achievements have taken place. While it is true that such a statement might preface the assessment of any nation's pre-modern era, it is particularly important that it does so in the case of the Japanese because the roots of so many contemporary cultural and educational values can be found in the history of this remarkable nation.

The most enduring influence of all is undoubtedly that of the Chinese civilization. By the beginning of the Heian period (794–1185) the Japanese had accepted and transformed the artistic and technical skills of Chinese craftsmen, had adopted and begun to change the Chinese script, had embraced and absorbed the religion of Buddhism and the philosophy of Confucianism and had built cities and temples in the Chinese style. Their first Education Code (701) was similarly Chinese in principle. It is true that Chinese studies languished somewhat between the Heian and Tokugawa eras but Tokugawa Ieyasu and his successors had no doubts concerning the importance of Confucianism in preserving, as a recent report puts it, 'respect for learning . . . respectful and benevolent hierarchical relationships, harmonious social relationships and morality' (Leestma *et al*, 1987, p. 1).

In many ways the Tokugawa period was as static as its rulers intended it to be but a number of unexpected developments, like the growth in power and wealth of the merchants, took place. It was to be expected that most of the sons of the *samurai* would be educated but it was not forseen that by the end of the era around 50 per cent of commoners would be attending school and that literacy levels in Japan would not be dissimilar to those in England and France (Dore, 1965, p. 291). By the same token it was not anticipated that commoners would place such a high value on education or be so ready to make financial sacrifices to ensure their children's attendance at school. (It is noteworthy that it is precisely this kind of parental interest and investment in education that lies behind the remarkable educational achievements of modern Japan.) In other words, a war against illiteracy in Japan was won before battle was joined since the desire to improve their lot by gaining new skills and knowledge was widespread among commoners before the Meiji period began.

However, perhaps the most remarkable legacy of all from the Tokugawa era was that in the early Meiji period a government made up substantially of *samurai* opted *not* for a dual education system with separate *samurai* and commoner schools but for a single system offering a unified and universal education for all. This decision may seem inexplicable in the light of the class structure and the social distance between the classes in Tokugawa Japan except for one vital factor — the widespread acceptance on the part of the commoners and *samurai* alike of the prevailing social order. The acceptance of the status quo was, of course, encouraged in the teaching of the Confucian ethic in every school in the country so that the young Meiji government had no reason to fear, as many other governments have feared, that by establishing universal popular education it would be posing a threat to the future of Japanese society. Nevertheless it was a bold but wise step that ensured from the beginning that education in Japan would be not only unified and universal but also comprehensive.

2

Education from Meiji to MacArthur, 1867–1945

In 1853 Commodore Perry of the United States Navy arrived in Japanese waters aboard one of four 'black ships', delivered a letter from President Fillimore requesting a trade treaty, declared that he would return the following year and then sailed away, pointedly, within sight of the citizens of Edo. This polite but impressive power play had an immediate effect on the shogunate. It perceived clearly that Japanese isolationism was at an end and that there was little point in taking on the Americans since the latter's naval supremacy was self-evident. Most Japanese had never so much as imagined the existence of steam ships let alone seen them, but one sighting was enough. The food supplies of Edo arrived chiefly by sea and the results of a blockade by more black ships the following year could not be contemplated. Although the *Bakufu* put on a brave face and constructed extra gun batteries in Edo Bay, its actual policy was to maintain peace at almost any cost and to delay the signing of a treaty for as long as possible. In the event, however, Perry returned in February 1854, brooked no prevarication and signed a treaty on 31 March 1854 at the village of Yokohama. Three years later, in December 1857, the newly installed diplomatic representative of the United States, Townsend Harris, after exercising the same sort of determination as his compatriot Perry, gained a unique audience with *Shogun* Tokugawa Iesada. The Americans had truly arrived and Japanese isolation from the rest of the world had ceased.

In August 1945 the headquarters of the American Eighth Army were set up at Yokohama and on 2 September 1945 on the deck of an American battleship in Tokyo Bay, General Douglas MacArthur, Supreme Commander for the Allied Powers (SCAP), watched as a Japanese delegation signed a formal surrender document. The General was aware that some parallels existed between his own position and that of Commodore Perry's but he was, perhaps, slow to realize that to the

Japanese he came to resemble more the reincarnation of a Tokugawa *shogun* than a *samurai* general. Certainly things happened quickly under MacArthur. Within a month in 1946 a group of American experts assessed the Japanese educational system and issued a report suggesting major changes all of which had been culled from the American system of co-educational and comprehensive schools. It is unlikely that these same experts anticipated the remarkable academic achievements that would follow from their recommendations or that 40 years on another group of American experts would visit Japan to discover how the conquered, using the same educational framework as the conquerors, could so convincingly outperform them.

The purpose of this chapter is to describe the development of education from the Meiji restoration to the arrival of MacArthur, but first it is necessary to explain something of the Meiji restoration itself.

The Meiji restoration (1868)

From the time of the audience of Townsend Harris with Tokugawa Iesada in December 1857 there followed ten years of confusion in which the powers of the shogunate could be seen to be wasting away. The inability of the *Bakufu* to resist the demands of the United States, Russia, Great Britain and France was demonstrated most clearly in several unequal trade treaties entered into with those countries in the name of the *shogun*. Retribution by extreme nationalists on the author of the treaties, one Ii Naosuke, soon followed, for he was assassinated in 1860 as his palanquin approached what is now the Imperial Palace in Tokyo. However, rectifying the actual treaties was a much longer process and became a preoccupation of Japanese foreign policy until the end of the century. The decline of the shogunate was further demonstrated in 1862 when the ancient rule prohibiting the family of a *daimyo* from leaving Edo when their master returned to his fief, in effect treating the *daimyo*'s family as hostages to its lord's good conduct, was abolished. The end finally came in January 1868 when an alliance of western clans overcame the army of the last *shogun* in a three-day battle outside Kyoto. Ironically, the battle that marked the passing of feudalism and the coming of the modern era also marked the revenge of the Western clans who had been defeated in a similar battle 250 years earlier by Tokugawa Ieyasu.

With the Tokugawa era at an end the youthful Emperor Meiji, who had ascended the Chrysanthemum throne just weeks before the final decisive battle, became the natural symbol for the new age. The restoration of imperial power was thus accomplished but in his 'Charter Oath' in April 1868 the young emperor expressed the policy of the ruling oligarchy of new men from the Western clans: 'Knowledge shall be sought throughout the world so as to strengthen the foundation of imperial rule' (quoted in Nishi, 1982, p. 12). Thus at the emperor's command Westernization in the nineteenth century proceeded with the same zeal as had characterized Sinonization in earlier centuries. A government-inspired mission headed by Prince Iwakura was dispatched to North America and Europe to discover the secrets of Western industrial success and, in addition, thousands of emissaries and private individuals travelled the world intent on bringing home the means whereby their country could catch up with the West's industrial development. It was apparent that the arduous years of *samurai* education had paid off, for the minute study of Chinese classics served as an excellent preparation for indefatigable note-taking and endless questioning of officials and engineers. Furthermore, the Confucian respect for learning ensured that what the travelling *samurai* were told and taught was recorded with such accuracy, borne home with such care and copied with such enthusiasm that in the first 20 years of the Emperor Meiji's reign 'the entire apparatus of Western material civilization seemed to find some reproduction, some kind of echo, in Japan' (Storry, 1976, p. 107).

Thus, seeking knowledge of an essentially practical kind became the hallmark of the Meiji restoration and led to the rapid abandonment of feudalism. In 1871, in the wake of the victory of the western clans over the shogunate, the territorial lords surrendered their fiefs and their commoners to the imperial power, for it was inconceivable that land that was rightfully the emperor's should be held by others and that people who were first and foremost subjects of the emperor should be ruled by lords. In 1873 the feudal military service of the *samurai* was replaced by national conscription because the western clans had demonstrated beyond contradiction that in their armies townsmen and countrymen could be trained to fight as effectively as any *samurai* warrior. But conscription of itself was not the key to the new age. It was recognized on all sides that the way forward was universal and comprehensive education. As General Yamada Kengi put it after returning from the European leg of the Iwakura mission:

> the foundation for a strong army is not simply a matter of giving arms to soldiers but rather to provide an education for the people as a whole, without distinction between town and country, and to give the people throughout the whole nation knowledge and learning without discrimination of class or rank (see Passin, 1965, p. 65).

Education from 1872 to 1890

The first Education Act, the Fundamental Code, of the new imperial government was issued in 1872. It represented a triumph for liberal views over the conservatives who would have continued the tradition of the Tokugawa period with its emphasis on ancient Chinese studies and the restriction of commoners' education to elementary schools. The chief proponent of liberal education in 1872 was Fukuzawa Yukichi (1835–1901). The 'Great Enlightener' was one of the most influential thinkers of his day and his report on Western schools (*Seiyo Jijo*) which was published in 1866 and was based on his visit to France in 1862, became immensely popular. Fukuzawa did not aspire to public office because he considered it important that some thinkers stayed outside government in order to appraise its actions more effectively. To this end he founded a school of Western learning (Keio Gijuku) which later became a leading private university, and he started a newspaper (*Jiji Shimpo*) in the modern tradition of independent journalism.

Fukuzawa's views on education find their fullest expression in his 'Encouragement of Learning' (*Gukumon No Susume*) which, like the first Education Act of the Meiji era, was published in 1872. In his book Fukuzawa asserts his belief in the essential equality of people at birth and explains later inequalities largely in terms of the degree to which individuals study to obtain knowledge. This view seems to be widely supported in modern Japan. Yamamura (1986, p. 37), for example, concludes from his studies of Japan's notorious examination system that 'parents' and teachers' strong emphasis on effort implies a belief in equality at birth, with success or failure entirely dependent on how hard the child tries'. It is difficult to imagine a more powerfully motivating belief than that effort will bring its own reward and for this reason it is likely to exist everywhere among those who seek to encourage learning but it would seem that it is in Japan, supremely, that this belief is widely held, lovingly transmitted and conscientiously practised.

Fukuzawa goes on to describe the sort of studies that are most likely to bring about a new equality between the social classes in the Meiji era. He acknowledges that studying the Chinese classics has its value and brings pleasure to the student, but he thinks that this type of 'unpractical' learning is not suited to the new age. Rather it is practical learning (*jitsugaku*) that is the order of the day. In addition to the three Rs, the curriculum should include bookkeeping and the use of scales as well as geography, natural philosophy, history, economics and ethics. Furthermore, Fukuzawa believed that translations of Western texts should be used in order to study these subjects.

Fukuzawa hoped that this Westernized and practical course of study would open the way for the advancement of all people of talent, irrespective of rank. Indeed, he entertained a vision of a well-ordered and harmonious society in which ignorance and illiteracy would be banished and where the government would be able 'to rule more easily and the people to accept its rule agreeably, each finding his place and helping to preserve the peace of the nation' (Passin, 1965, p. 209).

Certainly in contemporary Japan, where a very high literacy rate is accompanied by a quite remarkably low crime rate, important aspects of Fukuzawa's vision have been realized.

The Preamble to the Fundamental Code of 1872 expressed a liberal view of education similar to that of Fukuzawa's. It contained the same emphasis on learning as the key to success in life and a similar statement on the debilitating effects of ignorance. It extolled the virtues of the three Rs for all classes and criticized the 'evil' tradition of education for *samurai* only. Thus *every* person was enjoined to pursue learning and *every* guardian was commanded to make sure his children attended school so that in the future there should be 'no community with an illiterate family nor a family with an illiterate person' (Kobayashi, 1976, p. 25). However, it was one thing to plan for a universal, compulsory and comprehensive education system, it was quite another to bring it about.

The administrative model that appealed to the young Meiji leaders was the French one since it offered a centralized system under the control of a ministry of education. However, although centralization in curricular matters seemed highly desirable to the young leaders, centralized financial control did not. They thought that since it was self evident that the proposed new system of education would lead to the future prosperity and well-being of the people of Japan then the people of Japan should pay for it. This decision bore particularly hard on the rural peasantry, whose rents were still high after the abolition of feudalism and who now had to pay for their children's education in the form of both school fees and other compulsory contributions. It is likely that before the Meiji period education at the *terakoya* in more rural areas had been free or at least had been paid for in kind. Payment had depended on whether schools were provided by charitably disposed local dignitaries or by professional teachers. In both cases gifts would be presented to the teacher at appropriate times and festivals but, in the latter case, the community would provide the teacher with a living according to the means of individual villagers. Financial matters were conducted with great tact and delicacy and fixed sums of money were rarely discussed (Dore, 1965, p. 260). Thus in villages throughout Japan a subtle web of social relationships supported the *terakoya* at which attendance was voluntary and at which a curriculum was provided which suited local needs. It is not difficult to understand, therefore, the reaction of rural folk at the arrival of imposed central government schools offering a curriculum derived from Western texts and demanding fees and compulsory attendance. Not only was there much resentment at and absenteeism from the new schools in the early Meiji period (1872–1880) but also many school buildings, together with police stations and town halls, were burnt down by angry peasants.

The response of central government to these disturbances, as far as education was concerned, was not to subsidize the costs of the new elementary schools to any great extent but to instruct local bodies, both prefectural and municipal, to provide the funds for new schools. In fact some enthusiastic prefectural governors had anticipated the new code of education and had attempted to deal with the resulting financial difficulties. For example, Kobayashi (1976, p. 26) reports how Governor Nagayama of Chikuma toured his prefecture (*ken*) to encourage the building of schools and how both he and his officials made considerable contributions out of their own pockets. By contrast, central government funding for local initiatives between 1880 and 1910 never rose above 15 per cent of the national educational budget. (Passin, 1965, p. 70).

The Fundamental Code divided the country into 53,760 elementary school, 256 middle school and 8 university districts. Work started immediately on the elementary school programme since it was believed that without establishing a firm foundation to the educational system, there was little point in attempting to construct an edifice of middle schools and universities. In 1873, within a year of the promulgation of the Code, 12,500 primary schools had been opened and within five years this number had doubled to match contemporary levels of provision. However, an 1875 survey revealed that fewer than 20 per cent of the 'new' schools were in fact custom-built and that the majority of elementary schools were housed in existing buildings such as Buddhist temples, private houses and public buildings: even some warehouses were pressed into use (Passin, 1965, p. 74). In 1885 attendance levels at the new schools were running at only 50 per cent, with boys outnumbering girls by a ratio of two to one. (Kaigo, 1968, p. 65). Indeed, it was not until the early twentieth century that attendance levels for both sexes rose to over 90 per cent.

The Fundamental Code made provision for normal schools for the training of teachers but at first the financial rewards of the profession were so low that output from the training institutions was limited. Consequently, in the early years of the Meiji period the majority of teachers comprised untrained former *terakoya* staff, public-spirited citizens and educated *samurai*. However, it is the preponderance of *samurai* in the teaching force in the early years of the Meiji period that demands some explanation.

Both the peasantry and the *samurai* suffered financially as a result of the abolition of feudalism. The peasants' hardship was caused by high rents and school fees and the *samurai*'s by a small state pension that was later commuted to a small lump sum. Many *samurai*, of course, succeeded handsomely as a result of the Meiji restoration by becoming bureaucrats or entrepreneurs in the new order but as a class they were simply too large for all to succeed. It is estimated that in 1870 there were nearly 2 million *samurai* out of a population of 34 million (Storry, 1976, p. 108). This meant that there were thousands of former warriors who were finding it difficult to make ends meet and who had to face yet another blow to their pride. Ancient *samurai* traditions were swept away when a new decree allowed only policemen or members of the armed forces to carry swords and when the introduction of conscription clearly implied that all Japanese, regardless of birth, were capable of achieving martial skills that had for centuries been the birthright of the *samurai* alone. As with the peasants so with the *samurai*: frustration led to revolt.

The most serious revolt was led by Saigo Takamori, who was a member of the ruling oligarghy in the early Meiji period. His preferred foreign policy was to force open the trade gates of Korea in much the same way as Commodore Perry had forced Japan into trade with the United States. However, Japanese approaches to Korea were rebuffed and the majority of the members of the oligarchy were not disposed to back Takamori in an overseas adventure that was more likely to lead to conflict with Russia than to bring a final hour of glory to the *samurai* community. So Takamori withdrew from the oligarchy and returned to his home province of Satsuma, where he established a school in which martial arts were to the fore of the curriculum. However, he brooded on the changing fortunes of the *samurai* class and feared increasingly as they lost their right to carry swords and to be the sole military class that they would never again be the backbone of Japanese society. Finally, in 1877, Takamori rose in bloody revolution which, with great loss of life on both sides, was put down by a government conscript force. In the event there could have been no clearer demonstration of the fighting capability of the new Japanese army and the changing position in society of many of the *samurai*. It is perhaps no surprise, then, that those *samurai* who could not obtain positions in government business or sword-carrying occupations such as the army and the police turned to the one honourable profession still open to them. Teaching, which was still regarded as more of a heavenly calling than a common or garden profession and which was indisputably untainted by trade, was crying out for recruits. The dispossessed *samurai* responded to the call in great numbers.

In the early years of the Meiji period teachers of *samurai* origin were found in elementary schools in all parts of the country. Indeed, in some districts they made up a considerable proportion if not the whole of the teaching force. Similarly, in the normal schools *samurai* graduates outnumbered commoners by a ratio of at least two to one. Passin (1965, p. 77) notes that 'of the 240 graduates of the elementary school division of the Tokyo Normal School between 1873 and 1878, 164 were of *samurai* origin, 1 was of court noble origin and 75 were of commoner origin'. However, it is clear that by the end of the nineteenth century the teaching profession had lost much of its appeal to displaced warriors and that by the early years of the twentieth century ambitious young commoners were increasingly taking the places of the *samurai* in the normal and elementary schools. At the same time teaching came to be seen less as a heavenly calling and more as a rather lowly occupation, although by the end of the nineteenth century it could command a reasonable salary. Changes in the social status of teachers and the standing of the profession are clearly linked to the long and difficult gestation period of nearly 50 years between the announcement in 1872 of ambitious plans for state education and the final flowering in the 1920s of a system that produced 'the most highly literate people in Asia' (Storry, 1976, p. 113).

In 1872 only a minority of the teachers, perhaps one-sixth, had been trained, and therefore the heterogeneous group of volunteers that assembled in the first state elementary schools resorted in most cases to time-honoured methods of instruction. New textbooks, like new buildings, were in short supply and so old texts continued to be used. Even when new texts arrived they were not readily understood because they dealt with unfamiliar topics such as science and arithmetic and they employed Arabic numerals. It seems likely that some volunteer teachers may have side-stepped the question of understanding the new texts by getting pupils to recite passages from the new texts without any respect for their meaning. This practice is reminiscent both of rote learning (*sodoku*) experienced by the *samurai* in the Tokugawa period as they laboured to master the Chinese classics and of much preparation for examinations in Japan today.

In retrospect it can be seen that the use of Western texts in translation in Japanese schools immediately following the publication of the Fundamental Code of 1872 was an emergency measure only. Complaints that the texts were too difficult, too expensive and too remote from the lives of Japanese children led to their gradual abandonment. At the same time a more conservative approach to education was developing and there was an increasing desire for books to be based on Japanese culture and philosophy, particularly in the area of morals. In 1880 an inspection of textbooks began and a number were removed from circulation, including four that had been sanctioned by the Ministry of Education in 1872. In 1883 the first of the new indigenous texts on morals was published reflecting both a new position for moral teaching in the elementary school curriculum and a return to more Confucian principles in education.

Another indicator of the changing political climate can be found both in the revisions that were made to the Fundamental Code of 1872 and in conservative reaction to those provisions. The Educational Ordinance of 1879 was, if anything, more liberal than the original code. It recommended devolution rather than centralization in curriculum matters so that schools could be more responsive to the needs and interests of local people. To this end teacher autonomy was to be encouraged, textbooks simplified, compulsory education reduced to 16 months between the ages of 6 and 14 and corporal punishment brought to an end. This ordinance was the work of Education Minister Tanaka, who had been appointed in 1873. It clearly marks a watershed in the development of educational philosophy in Japan. Tanaka had brought an American professor, David Murray, to Japan to advise him during the heady years of 1873–1878 and in 1876 Murray and Tanaka visited the United States. Tanaka brought back materials ranging from school furniture to elementary readers as well as ideas of decentralization and teacher autonomy imbibed from the American school system. However, Tanaka's liberalism and Western ideas caused conservative hackles to rise.

In 1878 the young Emperor Meiji visited a number of provincial schools and was dismayed by what he saw. He observed that the influx of Western ideas had led to the sons of farmers and merchants discussing novel theories and using foreign words that could not be translated into Japanese. He feared for the future of traditional Japanese values and on his return issued an Imperial Rescript entitled 'The Great Principles of Education' (*Kyogaku Taishi*). This statement of conservative principles, which made clear that Westernization had gone too far and that there should be a return to Confucian principles, could not have come from a higher source. It was as if the Queen of England herself had personally intervened in the debate concerning the Education Reform Bill in 1988. However, the Imperial Rescript of 1879 had in fact been drafted by one Matoda Eifu, a Confucian lecturer and adviser to the emperor. This meant that when Ito Hirobumi, one of the founding oligarchs of the Meiji restoration and by no stretch of the imagination a liberal, was ordered to adjust Tanaka's Education Ordinance in the light of the Imperial Rescript he objected most forcefully, not so much on educational grounds but on the grounds that to allow a meddling Confucian adviser to dictate national policy would be to allow a most unwholesome precedent to occur. Consequently, Ito Hirobumi promulgated Tanaka's Education Ordinance and abolished the post of Confucian Lecturer to the Emperor. This victory, however, was short-lived. The Revised Education Ordinance of 1880 bore the stamp of Matoda's ideas and Tanaka was obliged to resign. The teaching of morals moved to the top of the curriculum and nothing more was heard of devolution or teacher autonomy. Indeed, in the view of the new Minister for Education, Kono, teachers were not independent scholars but guardians of morality and officers of the state. The Memorandum for Elementary School Teachers, issued in 1881, spelt this out:

Loyalty to the Imperial House, love of country, filial piety towards parents, respect for superiors, faith in friends, charity towards inferiors, and respect for oneself constitute the Great Path of human morality. The teacher must himself be a model of these virtues in his daily life, and must endeavour to stimulate his pupils along the path of virtue (quoted in Passin, 1965, p. 85).

Furthermore, in 1880 teachers' political freedoms were reduced when they were forbidden to attend political meetings or lectures. This ban betrayed a nervousness on the part of the government in the early Meiji period which was understandable in the light of the preceding centuries under the shogunate, when it had been assumed that all political gatherings were seditious in intent and that no distinction could be drawn between political opposition and treachery. Even so, it was announced in 1881 that some kind of national assembly would be instituted in 1890; and when, in 1889, the Prime Minister, Count Kuroda, received the first written constitution of Japan from the hands of the emperor, a modest step was taken in the direction of parliamentary democracy.

Interestingly, in 1878, as Englishwoman in her mid-forties, Isabella Bird, spent several months in Japan travelling on foot, horseback and even cow along 'unbeaten tracks'. She made a point of staying in villages and tiny settlements so that she could participate in everyday life. She was thus in a position to make a number of observations about children and schools. For example, in a village near Nikko she heard the drumbeats at 7 o'clock in the morning which summoned the children to a school housed in buildings which 'would not discredit any school-board at home' (Bird, 1984, p. 71). Bird thought that the school apparatus was of a good standard and that the maps were particularly fine. The young male teacher also impressed her with his energy and enthusiasm, as did the children with their unquestioning obedience. However, she noted that the older pupils were reading geographical and historical books aloud in a most disagreeable high pitch; she was also disturbed to see children working for hours at the Chinese classics in order to gain a minimal grasp of their meaning, despite the fact that officially the classics had been displaced from their central position in Japanese education. At the same time, Bird noted that some arithmetic and natural philosophy had been introduced into the curriculum of the village school.

The school day officially finished at noon, but Bird was very much aware that in the evening the village buzzed with preparation for the next day's lessons. Another evening activity observed by Bird was that of children reading popular stories about heroes and heroines of bygone days. The stories were obtained from circulating libraries which, according to Bird's account, were commonly found in villages in 1878.

Bird also visited the normal school in Kubota, which she described as 'the finest of the public buildings' (Bird, 1984, p. 163). Indeed, she was surprised by the quality of the equipment in the classrooms and, particularly, by the splendid apparatus in the laboratories.

Bird's testimony to the progress of education in the post-Meiji period is impressive. Her observations indicate that by the end of the first decade some well-equipped buildings had been erected and some progress had been made in modernizing the elementary school curriculum. But Bird also noticed what many subsequent visitors to Japan found — that there seemed to be a widespread ambition for educational success and also a method of childrearing that supported this ambition and thus the work of the schools and the teachers. She found, for example, that even in the school holidays the hum of lessons was audible along the street of the village for an hour every day. This was because the children had been set holiday tasks in preparation for an examination that they would take as soon as school reopened. Bird also found the docile and obedient behaviour of Japanese village children quite remarkable when compared with what she remembered of their brawling and disobedient English counterparts. On the other hand, she missed seeing truly impulsive behaviour and found that three-year-old Japanese children in kimonos and girdles were almost too formal and precocious to be true. Nevertheless, Bird acknowledges that in the villages the children were enjoyed and worshipped by their parents in a way that was not commonplace in the West — Bird had also visited the United States in the 1850s and so was able to make some comparisons. Perhaps most striking of all, however, was Bird's impression that filial piety and unquestioning obedience were the most common and the most highly valued attributes in the young. Indeed, Bird (1984, p. 198) claimed that she never saw 'a child troublesome or disobedient'. Since these very same characteristics were observed to lead to maximum effort at school, there exists in embryonic form in Bird's letters an early statement of the thesis that the twin pillars of child-rearing practice and educational success in Japan are ineluctably linked. A century later, Benjamin Duke (1986) and Merry White (1987) visited Japan for extended periods and developed this thesis, to which we shall return in Chapter 4.

Ito Hirobumi, before crossing swords with Matoda Eifu, had visited Europe in the 1860s and had been impressed by British mercantile and industrial might and by the German constitution, where the powers of an elected assembly were restricted by an executive responsible to the sovereign. The first convinced Ito that Japan was as yet in no position to do battle with the West, and the second led Ito to take control of the drafting of the new constitution and to ensure that power remained in the hands of those advising the emperor. Ito succeeded in retaining considerable power himself and when in 1885 he became the first prime minister of the modern era he appointed Mori Arinori as minister of education.

Mori Arinori, who had been Japan's first chargé d'affaires in the United States before transferring to Britain as consul, met Ito Hirobumi in Paris in 1882. The two shared their educational philosophies and found themselves so much in agreement that Ito promised Mori there and then that he would be Minister for Education. In the event he occupied that position for four important years (1885–1889) during which he experienced continuous opposition from the Emperor's Confucianist advisers led by the same Matoda who had drafted 'The Great Principles of Education'.

Nevertheless, Mori's achievements included the Elementary School Ordinance of 1886, which extended compulsory education to four years, and the Middle School Ordinance of 1887, which decreed that one such school should be established in every prefecture. However, up to half the child population could not attend for four compulsory years of elementary education because the facilities were not available, so a simplified three-year half-day course was all that many young pupils experienced until this stopgap measure was phased out in 1890. Similarly a middle school education was out of the reach of most young people at this time because places were so limited. For the academically able but poor even the offer of support from a generous merchant or former *daimyo* had to be weighed against the immediate loss of labour and earnings to the protégé's family. Consequently, as Kaigo (1968, p. 81) points out, 'most of the students who progressed to middle school were children of the families who had been warriors of the old clans'. By 1890, 55 middle schools were attended by 11,620 students but the students were all male and came from the middle and upper classes; according to Kaigo (1968, p. 81), 'the children of the general citizens were not permitted to enter the schools'.

However, it was Mori's policy for normal schools which proved to be the most controversial. A significant influence on this policy was the Swedenborgian, Thomas Lake Harris. Mori and a number of other Japanese students in the United States in 1867 had stayed at Harris's Utopian colony and had fallen under his spell. They had lived according to the principles of obedience to God, represented on earth by Harris, and a tough regime of discipline and physical fitness. When he became minister for education, Mori translated these ideals into a policy for normal schools where the students, who were supported by the state, were to experience a military-style discipline. Indeed, in Tokyo an army officer, Colonel Yamakawa, became head of the normal school where the inculcation of Dignity, Friendship and Obedience, three slogans borrowed by Mori from Harris, were the objectives of a physical fitness regime that included six hours of military drill each week. The emperor himself, of course, became the transcendental being to whom all obedience was ultimately directed.

By contrast with the normal schools and their emphasis on morality and nationalism, Mori established a university sector where academic freedom and critical analysis were to be positively encouraged. In effect Mori was attempting to channel the sceptical approach to learning favoured in the West into the university sector alone, in the knowledge that it was a necessary part of Western technological development but in the hope that it could be contained by an educated elite who would in any case have been thoroughly indoctrinated during their own passage through school.

Puzzles remain over the true nature of Mori's beliefs but the fact remains that the fanatical nationalist who assassinated him on 11 February 1889, the day of the promulgation of the new constitution, believed him to be too Westernized for the good of Japan. However, Mori, who had set education on a course it was to follow until 1947, might well have approved of the resurgence of conservatism and nationalism expressed in the Imperial Rescript on Education issued in 1890.

The official translation into English of the Imperial Rescript on Education was issued by the Ministry of Education in 1909 and it reads as follows:

> Know ye, Our subjects:
> Our Imperial Ancestors have founded our Empire on a basis broad and everlasting and have deeply and firmly implanted virtue; Our subjects ever united in loyalty and filial piety have from generation to generation illustrated the beauty thereof. This is the glory of the fundamental character of Our Empire, and herein also lies the source of Our education. Ye, Our subjects, be filial to your parents, affectionate to your brothers and sisters; as husbands and wives be harmonious, as friends true; bear yourselves in modesty and moderation; extend your benevolence to all; pursue learning and cultivate arts, and thereby develop intellectual faculties and perfect moral powers; furthermore advance public good and promote common interest; always respect the Constitution and observe the laws; should emergency arise, offer yourselves courageously to the State; and thus guard and maintain the prosperity of Our Imperial Throne coeval with heaven and earth. So shall ye not only be Our good and faithful subjects, but render illustrious the best traditions of your forefathers. The Way here set forth is indeed the teaching bequeathed by Our Imperial Ancestors, to be observed alike by Their Descendants and the subjects, infallible for all ages and true in all places. It is Our wish to lay it to heart in all reverence, in common with you, Our subjects, that we may thus attain to the same virtue.

It is difficult to exaggerate the importance of the Rescript. It was promulgated by the emperor himself on 30 September 1890 and on the instructions of the Ministry of Education a copy was placed in every state school in the country. Sometimes the Rescript was housed in a small shrine, which served only to add to the sense of religious ritual when on ceremonial days the principal of the school solemnly withdrew it in order to read it aloud to the assembled pupils. The Rescript rapidly assumed the status of holy writ and became the nation's fundamental ethical code for the next 55 years. In common with most sacred writings it spawned hundreds of exegetical texts which attempted to elucidate its exact meaning and significance.

First and foremost, the Rescript claimed continuity with the past through the person of the emperor and his ancestors. In 1890, the official view was that the imperial line began with the sun-goddess Amaterasu, although one Jimmu Tennu was accepted as the 'human' founder of the dynasty in 660 BC. The 2,600th anniversary of this event was solemnly commemorated in front of the Imperial Palace in Tokyo in November 1940 and until 1945 the ancient myths concerning both the divine origin and the human founding of the imperial house were taught as spiritual truths if not historical facts in Japan's elementary schools. Indeed, until the end of the Pacific War any scholar who was inclined to question the historicity of these events on the entirely reasonable grounds that valid evidence was lacking, risked committing the crime of *lèse-majesté* and losing his job.

Second, the writers of the Rescript, like Tokugawa Ieyasu three hundred years before, recognized the value of Confucianism in securing the hearts and minds of the Japanese people. Thus the Rescript is suffused with Confucian ideals such as filial piety, obedience and benevolence which the children of Japan were solemnly adjured to observe. In truth it was but a very short step from the sacred text of the Rescript to the recommendations in the textbooks for the teaching of morals in schools that loyalty to the emperor and loyalty to one's parents were one and the same thing. As Smith (1983, p. 16) comments, 'the household and the state had been effectively encapsulated into an indivisible sacred entity of sentiment and ceremony'.

The conservative reaction, then, to the influx of Western ideas that characterized the opening of the Meiji era, was embodied supremely in the Imperial Rescript on Education. As Rohlen (1983, p. 52) has observed, the Ministry of Education intended to establish in the Rescript the notion that Japanese morality and values were equally as significant as Western science and technology and that Japanese social loyalties and practices were basic to the new system of education. In other words, the Rescript was intended to 'japanize' Western influences in the nineteenth and twentieth centuries just as effectively as

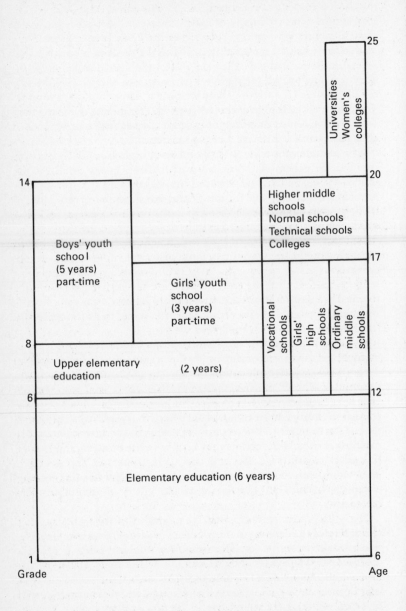

Figure 1 The Japanese educational system before 1945

Chinese influences had been assimilated in earlier centuries. It has to be said that with the Emperor Meiji providing the essential link between the present and the past and with Confucianism under-pinning moral and nationalistic aspirations, the limpid prose of the Rescript achieved its aims to a quite remarkable degree.

Education from 1890 to 1945

If the first half of the Meiji era (1869–1890) saw the rise of compulsory, coeducational and comprehensive elementary education, then the sec-ond half (1890–1912) saw the development of a secondary education that was essentially elitist. The Fundamental Code of 1872 had envis-aged three levels of education — elementary, middle and higher — but numerous practical difficulties prevented the realization of these ambitious plans beyond the elementary level much before the end of the emperor's long reign. However, in the city of Kyoto in 1868, four years before the Fundamental Code was issued, plans were already being made for two middle schools for the graduates of elementary schools who wished to proceed to university. These two middle schools would allow 16-year-olds to study in the specialized areas of law, letters, science, medicine and teaching that would be open to them when at the age of 22 they entered university.

Kyoto's example in establishing middle schools was soon followed by Tokyo in 1870; thereafter, reinforced by the recommendations of the Fundamental Code, middle school education slowly developed throughout Japan. According to the Code there was to be a tripartite system of secondary education comprising ordinary middle schools, vocational schools and evening schools. The first were to number 256 and were to provide a general education for those who had successfully graduated from elementary school; the second were not to be estab-lished immediately but were to offer technical, commercial, agricul-tural and foreign language education; the third were intended for work-ing people but were little more than pipe dreams in 1872 since no concrete plans existed for their foundation. The first, the ordinary middle schools, were to be organized into two divisions and were the precursors of today's junior and senior high schools.

In the early Meiji years, however, the term 'middle school' was used quite loosely to describe any establishment that provided post-elementary education. Thus a Ministry of Education report issued in 1875 recorded the existence of 116 middle schools, although only 11 of these could be described as district middle schools in the meaning of the Fundamental Code (Kaigo, 1968, p. 78). The rest were private schools, of which 80 per cent were located in Tokyo. So it remains true, as we have already observed, that three years after Mori Arinori's Middle School Ordinance of 1887 only 55 of the 256 prefectures possessed middle schools. Many of these 55 prefectural schools were in fact the old *han* or fief schools that had been built in the Tokugawa period for the education of *samurai* boys. Since the new prefectures followed the lines of the former Tokugawa feudal domains it was not difficult to reform and rename the fief schools to fit the requirements of the Fundamental Code. At first Western teachers were brought in to handle some of the new subjects — e.g. foreign languages, mathematics, geography, natural science, physics, chemistry and physical education — but not all the old traditions of the fief schools were so easily changed. There were continuities from the Tokugawa era into the Meiji era both in teaching staff and in the expectation that the brightest graduates of the middle schools would enter public service. This explains, in a nutshell, why middle school education from 1890 to 1945 was elitist and male-dominated. It was in effect the direct heir to the education of the *samurai* of the Tokugawa period but with one important additional ingredient. It was no longer sufficient for a boy simply to come from a 'good' family, he had also to go to a 'good' school and, above all, to reach a high standard of academic achievement. His sister, however, enjoyed a very different kind of educational experience that did not fit into any of the three categories of the official tripartite system.

The prefectural middle schools were not coeducational and so girls whose parents wished them to continue their education beyond elementary school were obliged to attend specially designated high schools. The first government-sponsored girls' high school was established in Tokyo in 1871; by 1895 there were 15 high schools for girls attended by nearly 3000 pupils; and by 1945 the number of schools had increased to 1272, with nearly 876,000 pupils (Kaigo, 1968, p. 85). In 1945, there were 776 prefectural boys' schools with 640,000 pupils enrolled; while there were at that time more prefectural schools for girls, with more girls enrolled, the education boys received was vastly superior in terms of academic content. Girls were taught science and mathematics in a simplified form and foreign languages not at all. The subjects they *were* taught included ethics for women, etiquette, home economics, the care of children, sewing and handicraft. No provision at all was made for girls to enter university. Doubtless there were noble and heroic exceptions to the above but in general girls who were able to obtain a secondary education were being prepared for the life of a housewife and for very little else. This may explain why it was not until 1899 that the entry requirements for the girls' high schools (completing six years' elementary school) were brought into line with those for boys' middle schools.

Vocational schools were also slow to develop. Although mooted in the Fundamental Code of 1872, it was not until industrial output began to rise in the 1890s that the need for an educated workforce became apparent. These apprentice schools, because that is in effect what they were, gave instruction in arithmetic, geometry, physics, chemistry and drawing as well as ethics; but specifically, students were trained for jobs in factories. Schools for farm workers were also set up particularly for use during the slack agricultural season. In 1899 the Vocational School Order institutionalized five types of school: technical, agricultural, commercial, mercantile marine and supplementary. Unlike the middle schools and the girls' high schools, entry to the vocational schools was open to any graduate of the elementary schools and, between 1890 when 2435 students attended 23 schools and 1945 when about 850,000 students attended 1743 schools, this route to secondary education became a significant second force. However, the vast majority of young people in Japan followed yet another route which in 1940 accounted for over 2.5 million students at 20,000 establishments (Kaigo, 1968, p. 88). Yet, curiously, despite these students being in their late teens at the completion of their course, they were deemed to have received an extended elementary education rather than a secondary education.

This popular route to 'secondary' education arose because in the last decade of the nineteenth century the modernization of industry in Japan gathered pace. This led both the government to redouble its efforts to remove illiteracy in order to gain a well-educated workforce and the Japanese people to educate their children better in order to maintain and, if possible, increase their newly found prosperity. Thus in 1907 the Elementary School Ordinance increased the number of years of compulsory education from four to six, while at about the same time elementary education became entirely free in all parts of the country. For their part, the children responded to six years of compulsory education by staying on in increasing numbers for an additional two years of upper elementary school. Thus the Meiji ideal of 'no family without primary education' was eventually realized over 50 years after the restoration when in 1925 for the first time some 99 per cent of the child population attended primary school. Furthermore, in the 1930s the pipe dreams of 1872, that evening classes for the children of workers be set up, were finally realized. Evening and Sunday classes for young people in work had existed from the 1890s but from 1935 graduates from the upper elementary schools could attend youth schools for five years if they were male and for three years if they were female. Finally, in 1939 the part-time evening youth schools became obligatory. One other voluntary route for education and training had existed since 1926 when the Ministry of Education and the Bureau of the Army set up military training institutes where young men from the age of 16 could receive part-time education in the evenings for four years. Of necessity, military drill formed a major part of this experience but tuition in vocational and general subjects also took place.

From the beginning to the end of the period from Meiji to MacArthur it was the ordinary middle schools that were the elite institutions. Their pupils were largely the children of the middle and upper classes who, after five years at ordinary middle school, hoped to enter one of 32 higher middle schools for a further three years. Only the most outstanding graduates of the ordinary middle schools, about 20 per cent, passed the entrance examinations to the higher middle schools and of these only the best reached university. Until 1870, when a second imperial university was established in Kyoto, Tokyo possessed the only imperial university. Since graduates of Tokyo University were virtually guaranteed prestige career positions at a national level, the most prized route to the top of the academic and occupational tree became defined as: Seishi Primary School in Hongo Ward, Tokyo, Tokyo First Middle School; Tokyo First Higher School; and Tokyo Imperial University (Passin,1965, p. 106). The means of proceeding to the middle and higher schools, aside from status and sex, was the entrance examination.

The entrance examination system introduced both *juken jigoku* or examination hell and, at the same time, 'the seeds of a meritocratic order' (Rohlen, 1983, p. 11) to Japanese education for it allowed hard-working and talented boys who were not from former *samurai* families to enter ordinary and higher middle schools and even the imperial universities. However, in 1935 only a small proportion of the population was interested in higher education and less than 3 per cent of all elementary school graduates attended university. Nevertheless, those students who completed higher middle school but did not enter university still found excellent jobs and graduates of ordinary middle schools who did not progress to higher middle school had no difficulty in finding managerial positions, for the middle schools with their distinctively broad and academically rigorous curricula represented mainline secondary education in pre-war Japan. Middle school graduates also had the option of attending technical institutes (*senmongakko*) which, by 1900, according to Shimahara (1979, p. 58) 'produced more than eight times as many skilled students as the imperial universities'. The vocational schools, on the other hand, represented a route that was considered more lowly because their graduates rarely obtained an advanced education and usually took jobs in industry. Furthermore, the jobs they took, however important in advancing industrial progress in Japan, were perceived as possessing a lower status than those of government officials and office workers.

It is tempting at this point to see what comparisons can be made by examining the major developments in English popular education for the period 1867–1945. The period is bounded by two major Acts of Parliament. The first, the 'Forster' Education Act of 1870, brought about universal elementary education, the second, the 'Butler' Act of 1944 did the same for secondary education. By 1893, elementary education in England and Wales had been made compulsory and free with the result that schools were better built, equipment more generously provided, teachers better paid and attendance higher than ever before. Indeed, such was the popularity of the new 'board' schools that in the larger towns and cities experiments had begun with higher grade schools which provided secondary education for elementary school pupils who wished to continue their studies. Interestingly, it had not occurred to legislators in 1870 that working-class children might wish to continue their education beyond the age of 12.

Secondary education for the children of the middle and upper classes had existed in England for several hundred years in public and grammar schools but at the beginning of the nineteenth century the academic and moral standards of these schools had sunk to an all-time low. Parents reacted by having their children educated at home by tutors and governesses or at the newly created private schools which offered modern curricula and close supervision of behaviour. However, due to the work of a group of reforming public school headmasters, the most famous of whom was Thomas Arnold of Rugby, this situation was completely transformed.

By the beginning of the twentieth century the reformed public schools, with their morning services, houses and sixth-formers and their liberal, literary and non-vocational curricula, had become powerful models especially for those founding a new generation of grammar schools. The only other possible models, the higher grade schools, came to an ignominious end.

The higher grade schools usually offered a vocational secondary education with a bias towards science and technology. Some schools entered their scholars for leaving examinations and a few students graduated from the higher grade schools and entered the local university college. There was much to be said for this new route up the educational ladder for it had become apparent at the Great Exhibition of 1851 and was confirmed at the Paris Exhibition of 1867 that, compared with the rapid advances in industrialization in Prussia, France and the United States, Britain was showing signs of relative decline. Furthermore, it was considered by many that the growing success of our competitors was due to the superiority of their secondary and technical education. However, in England the path for secondary education in the twentieth century was set by the 'Balfour' Education Act of 1902, which confirmed that the mainline route would be the literary and non-vocational grammar schools. By contrast, the vocational, technical and scientific route was curtailed although not completely cut off. The higher grade schools were to be replaced either by higher elementary schools with restricted curricula and a compulsory leaving age of 15 years or by trade (or junior technical) schools. In 1934 the latter numbered 194, with an attendance of 22,158 (Lowndes, 1969, p. 155). From 1907 onwards a new route was opened up for bright and ambitious elementary school children who in increasing numbers were able to sit scholarship examinations and gain free places at the local grammar school. This was a very English use of talent because, as Wardle (1970, p. 73) comments, 'a working class child who entered a grammar school was expected to take on the ethos of the middle class institution; he became *ex officio* a member of the middle class'. Essentially this solution was confirmed by the 'Butler' Education Act of 1944, for although 'parity of esteem' between the grammar schools and the new secondary modern schools was expressed in the Act as the hope of the legislators, it was never achieved and the grammar schools continued to be treated and regarded as superior in status to their poorer cousins, the descendants of the higher elementary schools.

In comparing the development of English and Japanese education for the period delineated by this chapter, a number of parallels suggest themselves. The first is the urgency in both countries to establish universal elementary education in the 1870s, the Japanese in order to catch up with the West, the British in order to regain the lead they had once had in industrial development. By the 1890s in England mass truancy from elementary schools had been overcome and attendance figures were similar to those of today, whereas in Japan the twentieth century had dawned before attendance reached modern levels. In both countries pupils voted with their feet and stayed on at elementary school beyond the statutory six years, but in Japan vocational education was developed and not curtailed. There are obvious similarities between the ordinary middle school of Japan and the grammar schools of England and Wales. Contest mobility existed in both countries because entrance examinations enabled some of those with ability but with lower social status to gain access to mainline secondary education. In England girls also were able to proceed through grammar school to university and so had better educational opportunities than their Japanese counterparts. In England the public school system enabled some children without great ability but who came from wealthy homes to enjoy the benefits of a prestigious secondary education. Naturally, in Japan also, wealthy parents were and still are able to buy private education for their children but, with some notable exceptions, the elite institutions have remained the government-sponsored schools and not the private or 'public' schools as they are confusingly called in England. In both countries entrance to the higher echelons of power depended crucially on attending a few highly selective schools and universities, but in Japan the importance of educating the whole population of young people to as high a standard as possible was seen and acted on earlier than in England. Thus in Japan in 1939 it was made obligatory for the 75–80 per cent of elementary school graduates who had not enrolled in secondary schools to continue with part-time education at the youth schools. Hence in 1941 most young men in Japan continued to receive some form of education until the age of 19 and most young women until 17. In England the demand for vocational or professional training was met most significantly by the development of the evening class route to the award of National Certificates but between 1922, when the scheme was initiated, and 1934 the total number of certificates and diplomas awarded was only 25,000 (Lowndes, 1969, p. 154). In England advances in education have been inhibited at various times by what Wardle (1970, p. 83) calls 'the chronic fear of over-educating the lower orders' as well as by the belief that a good liberal education is sufficient preparation for most major careers in the modern world. In Japan the need to master modern technology and to educate the workforce seems to have overcome the first of these English-style inhibitions, if in fact it ever existed, and to have modified the second.

By any standards the Meiji restoration of 1868 was a remarkable event and the decision of the new leaders to respond to the challenges of the West by educating their young people in Western and scientific thought was a momentous one. When the Emperor Meiji died in 1912 the development of universal elementary education was virtually complete and 'by 1941 most Japanese youth were actually staying in school on a part-time basis until the age of seventeen' (Rohlen, 1983, p. 60). In other words, the foundations had been laid for the remarkably high participation and low drop-out rates characteristic of contemporary Japanese education at all levels.

The Japanization of Chinese cultural influences was a distinctive feature of the pre-modern period and took place over centuries but quite remarkably, in education at least, the Japanization of Western scientific and technological influences was virtually complete in the first two decades of the Meiji era. Progress during these 20 years, however, was somewhat erratic and has been described by Shimahara (1979, p. 47) as 'a dialectical course of trial and error'. Three major documents of the period serve to illustrate Shimahara's statement. The first, the Fundamental Code of 1872, represented a conscious departure by the youthful oligarchy from centuries of *samurai* education and a positive embrace of French and American models of education but, by contrast, the second document, the Imperial Rescript, entitled 'The Great Principles of Education', issued by the court in 1879 after the young emperor had returned from visiting provincial schools, made clear that there should be a return to traditional principles because Westernization had gone too far. This rescript, which was drafted by the emperor's Confucian adviser, both *fore-*

shadowed the greater rescript of 1890 and overshadowed the last of the liberal education ordinances issued in 1879. The third document, the Imperial Rescript on Education of 1890, must be one of the most remarkable educational documents of all time. As Hardwick (1970, p. 74) comments, 'the rescript assumed almost sacred proportions in children's minds, with the result that in adulthood each would offer himself unhesitatingly and courageously to the state when called to do so'.

There were few signs in the last decade of the Meiji era that the loyalty of the graduates of the country's elementary schools would be put to the test and, even in 1926, when the grandchild of the Emperor Meiji, Hirohito, succeeded to the throne few doubted that the title of his reign, *Showa* or 'enlightened peace', was chosen with utter sincerity. However, as militarism gained strength against a background of public impatience with the inability of successive governments to deal with economic recession, ominous signs appeared. Prime Minister Hamaguchi, an honest and determined man, fell foul of the military and died after an assassination attempt in 1930 and in the following spring senior army officers seriously discussed a *coup d'état* as the country entered the decade known as the *Kurai tanima* or 'dark valley'.

The death of Emperor Hirohito in January 1989 reopened the debate about his role in these troubled years. Although he possessed immense prestige and was, in theory, the arbiter of all questions, he appears to have relied on the advice of various bodies such as the Cabinet, the general staff of the Army and Navy, and the Privy Council — who by no means agreed among themselves. But it is at least arguable that, had the emperor issued an imperial rescript on the pattern of his grandfather's or spoken *ex cathedra* as he did in 1945, then he might have halted military atrocities in Nanking and prevented his country's slide into the Pacific War. However, no public pronouncements were made, whatever the emperor may have said in private, and so the militarists gained virtual control of the country and the schools. The latter, despite all their fine achievements in the period under review, were compelled to foster nationalism and to give military training, and their end, as described by Kobayashi (1976, p. 40), was unmitigated chaos:

> In 1945, when the mainland of Japan was constantly under severe air attack, regular schooling became almost impossible. School buildings were either destroyed or utilized for war services. Children in large cities were forced to evacuate to the country. Young male teachers were all in military service. In March 1945 the government, almost in despair, declared an emergency in national education, by which all schooling except in national schools was to

be suspended temporarily to prepare the nation for the forthcoming final battle on the mainland. Japanese national education had thus been already defeated by this educational *hara-kiri* before two atomic bombs brought the tragic war to a miserable end for the people of Japan in August 1945.

3

Formal and non-formal education, 1945–1987

On 4 January 1946, General Douglas MacArthur, Supreme Commander for the Allied Powers (SCAP), sent a telegram to the USA War Department in Washington. It read 'Rehabilitation of Japanese educational system given high priority in occupation operations. Estimated 18 million students, 400,000 teachers, 40,000 schools represent major medium for influencing Japanese life' (Nishi, 1982, p. 189). MacArthur went on to request an education mission be sent to Japan because he felt the Japanese educators were unqualified to execute the task of initiating a complete reform of the education system. For good measure, he appended a list of 26 potential mission members. In early March 1946 ten of MacArthur's nominees arrived in Tokyo accompanied by fourteen additional members invited by the state department. They were presented with a booklet entitled *Education in Japan*, compiled by the Civil Information and Education Section, (CIE), General Headquarters (GHQ) SCAP, and asked to study it.

On 8 March 1946 the Minister for Education, Abe Yoshishige, welcomed the US mission and requested the members not to deal with Japanese education purely from an American point of view by imposing an alien culture on the defeated nation. This speech was listened to politely, but then the mission set about its predetermined task of replacing militaristic and nationalistic propaganda in Japanese schools with democratic organizational and educational innovations in the American tradition. As Rohlen (1983, p. 63) comments of the period in general: 'The Americans were sent to demilitarize and democratize Japan. Fresh from a global defeat of fascism they were a naïvely confident group that neither questioned the superiority of the American system nor understood much about Japan.' For two weeks the work of the mission consisted of attending morning lectures by CIE staff, afternoon field trips or committee meetings and evening entertainments. During the third and final week the chairman, George Stoddard, and Ernest R. Hilgard, later a professor of educational psychology at Stanford University, produced the report, entitled *Education for Democracy in Japan.*

The main recommendations of the report which led to direct action were, first, that there should be no more imperial rescripts on education and no more worship of imperial portraits; second, that compulsory schooling be extended from six to nine years; third, that Japanese teachers be unionized; and fourth, that local school boards be instituted. In fact many school officials, in anticipation of the report, had already secretly and reverently burned portraits of the emperor. In addition, they buried any misgivings they might have had about the new era in the face of the appalling practical difficulties that faced them. Most pressing was the fact that hungry and demoralized teachers presided over immensely large classes of undernourished children in a variety of settings, including the open skies. Indeed, about one-third of all existing schools lay in ruins. Conditions, therefore, were ripe for a remarkable experiment in what MacArthur described as the 'world's great laboratory' (Nishi, 1982, p. 41). The SCAP possessed unprecedented powers and, until his dismissal by President Truman in 1951, ruled as autocratically as any Tokugawa *shogun*. The Japanese people, for their part, were in no position to resist, for their country, which had never known defeat or experienced occupation, had now to come to terms with both. Furthermore, the emperor, whom they had believed to be divine, had spoken to them for the first time on the radio and told them that in the interests of peace for future generations they were to endure the unendurable and suffer the unsufferable.

In 1983 President Ronald Reagan and Prime Minister Yasuhiro Nakasone met in Tokyo and agreed that their countries should study each other's education systems since both countries were engaged in a process of reappraisal and educational reform. In the United States the need was seen to improve the quality of mathematics and science in schools and in Japan there was much concern to develop new levels of creativity in students so that the nation might maintain its lead in high-technology industries and further its enjoyment of economic success. The inquiries began in 1984 and the American report, entitled *Japanese Education Today* (Leestma et al.) was published in 1987.

This report, unlike that produced by the US Education Mission of 1946, was based on an extensive and sympathetic study of contemporary Japanese education in the context of its unique cultural and historical background. It acknowledged the high quality of Japanese compulsory education, the high level of student attainment and the high retention rate of students in that almost everyone completed 12 years' schooling. It noted that Japanese children were highly

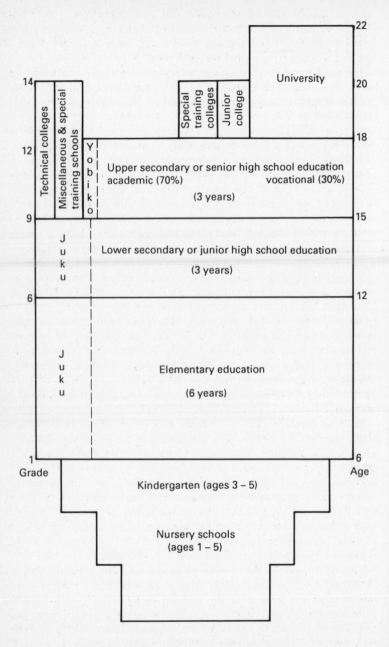

Figure 2 The Japanese educational system after 1947

motivated and well behaved, that their teachers were competent, respected and well paid, and that Japanese parents supported their children wholeheartedly and paid for pre-school, extra school and, if necessary, private school education. The report does not stand alone. The 1980s saw a spate of articles and books, both British and American, that praised the Japanese for their educational achievements, sought to understand the reasons for their success and hoped to discover what lessons could be learned for the writer's own country. Three recent book titles with their subtitles are perhaps sufficient to underline this point: *The Japanese School: Lessons for Industrial America* by Benjamin Duke (1986), *The Japanese Educational Challenge: A Commitment to Children* by Merry White (1987), and *Educational Achievement in Japan: Lessons for the West* by Richard Lynn (1988).

The purpose of this chapter is to attempt to explain the remarkable development of the formal education system in modern Japan as well as the informal system that grew up alongside it.

Post-war education reform, 1945–1952

As we have seen, education in pre-war Japan was characterized not only by a uniform elementary sector but also by a complex and hierarchical secondary sector comprising middle, vocational, higher elementary and youth schools. Generally speaking, only the middle school route led to higher education, therefore, there was much need of reform if equality of educational opportunity was to be extended to secondary education. In fact there had been much debate in the pre-war years on the improvement of the school system which had led to the 1941 National School Order. This Order included a regulation extending compulsory education by two years with effect from 1944, but because of the Pacific War the regulation was not put into effect.

In the aftermath of the war, on 15 September 1945, and within two weeks of the signing of the formal surrender document, the Ministry of Education published the 'Educational Plan for Building a New Japan'. The plan sought to anticipate SCAP directives on educational reform by recommending a new peaceful climate in schools in which militaristic thoughts would be disregarded and textbooks would be revised. The plan delicately explained, however, that 'due to the circumstances' deletions would have to be made in the textbooks currently in use. The 'circumstances' of post-war devastation certainly prevented the immediate production of new textbooks but did not prevent the plan calling for a new policy on scientific education. Indeed, on 18 August 1945, two weeks before the surrender was formalized, Maeda Tamon, the Minister for Education, in his inaugural address, made clear that the advancement of scientific education was at the top of his agenda. In Nishi's (1982, p. 61) opinion, one reason for this call for the expansion of scientific education was that the nuclear attacks on Japan had revealed a backwardness in the nation's scientific and technological development which was as significant in 1945 as the appearance off the Japanese coast in 1853 of Commodore Perry's black steamships. Certainly schemes were devised to award scholarships to students studying science, although in the circumstances of a nation living at a subsistence level such optimism for the future, however admirable, was hardly practical. Yet this very same impractical optimism and determination in the midst of devastation may be the key to our understanding of all that followed in the rebuilding of Japan.

The American response to Maeda's plan came first from the Research and Analysis Branch (R & A) of the State Department. R & A concluded that the plan revealed little change in Japanese attitudes except in respect to scientific training. It wondered, therefore, why there were no proposals to revise courses in Japanese ethics and history, since it was these courses that were the chief vehicles of militaristic propaganda. Maeda, however, knew nothing of these reactions to his plan when, on 13 October 1945, he was called in by CIE and handed a list entitled 'Concerning Change in Constitution of Ministry of Education'. These changes bore no relation to Maeda's plan and proposed instead, in the watchwords of the day, the decentralization and democratization of Japanese education. It was a bitter blow to Maeda that his own suggestions for voluntary change had been ignored, but worse was to follow. On 22 October 1945, MacArthur published his first educational directive, 'Administration of the Educational System of Japan'. It was a characteristically hard-hitting document which ordered the complete revision of all educational instruction in terms of democratic and peaceful government and the dignity and freedom of the individual. It insisted that students, teachers and the general public be fully informed about the part played during the war by their leaders as well as the part played by those who had passively acquiesced with the military government. This latter category appeared to include nearly all Japanese except those socialists and communists who had been imprisoned for political reasons. So MacArthur became, briefly, a champion of left-wing activists and at rather greater length a uniquely autocratic democratizer. In Beauchamp's (1987, p. 303) rather wooden words: 'One of the great ironies of this period was that in encouraging the democratization of Japanese education, the actions of the all-powerful occupation forces were often not democratic.'

The American hope and the Japanese fear was that a growth in individualism would nurture popular democracy and wither imperial sovreignty. However, for a people reared for decades on the ideals of the Emperor Meiji's Imperial Rescript on Education, in which public and private morality was seen as essentially one, the concept of individual freedom and responsibility in the political arena was frighteningly new. However, some groups in Japanese society were more ready than others to embrace the new democracy. First and foremost among them were the students.

It was the students of Mito High School who led the first post-war strike. They demanded from the Ministry of Education the dismissal of their authoritarian principal, and in little over a month the principal had gone and the strike was concluded. Shortly afterwards the president of the Peers' School, which the young Hirohito had attended, was also forced to resign. The flood of resignations which followed, from principals and teachers who had actively supported the military regime, encouraged high school and university students to become more vocal and to demand the return of liberal teachers and banned subjects like the social sciences. The students also campaigned for self-government and equal educational opportunities for women. In fact they became the spearhead for the educational changes demanded by MacArthur in his first educational directive. In vain did Ministry of Education officials appeal to the talisman that had served them for so long, the Imperial Rescript on Education of 1890 but nothing it seemed could prevent the restoration of academic freedom from taking place. Maeda was obliged not only to remove teachers who had been active supporters of the discredited regime but also to reinstate teachers who had been dismissed for political reasons. Some measure of the size of this movement can be gauged from the fact that, from the first student strike of September 1945 to the final agreement between CIE and the Ministry of Education on the screening of teachers in May 1946, 155,778 teachers and education officials resigned (Nishi, 1982, p. 173). The screening of nearly 1 million personnel continued until April 1949 with the loss of a further 3,000 supporters of the old régime. Also removed from schools were the propagation of Shintoism and the right to organize visits to Shinto shrines, though, interestingly, the latter is very much a feature of contemporary Japan. For an appraisal of this post-war period from the Japanese point of view Ishiguro's (1986) novel, *An Artist of the Floating World*, is warmly recommended.

The necessity for purging textbooks as well as the teaching profession was particularly acute because of the tradition in Japan of pupils memorizing their texts from beginning to end. The practice of learning by rote (*sodoku*) developed during the Tokugawa era and is still commonly found in modern Japan. It was understood from the earliest days of the occupation that textbook revision was high on the agenda but Japanese officials were as dismayed with the hard line taken by the Americans as the Americans were amazed at the contents of the textbooks in morals or *shushin*. Together with texts in Japanese history and geography, they were judged by the CIE to be pernicious, particularly since they represented almost one-third of all prescribed texts in schools and took up 15–20 per cent of all class time. In November 1945, the CIE ordered the Japanese educational printing presses to be stopped and the three 'pernicious' subjects to be proscribed and replaced by CIE courses of study. Offending textbooks were to be pulped and all new texts were to be translated into English and submitted to CIE for evaluation. This drastic action caused an acute shortage of textbooks at a time when there was already an acute shortage of paper as well as a formidable workload for the Ministry of Education. However, the CIE's orders were formalized by MacArthur into a directive on 31 December 1945 and it was understood that disobedience would not be dealt with lightly. The following day, 1 January 1946, the emperor formally renounced his divinity.

The purge of educational institutions begun by the Americans in 1945 signalled the end of a 20-year period in which dissenting voices had been systematically suppressed. For example, the student movement of the early 1920s, which had resulted in the formation of a federation of socialist students, had seen many of its leaders arrested and organizations dissolved between 1926 and 1930. Similarly the teachers' attempts to unionize themselves and liberalize education in the early 1930s were met with oppression and suppression. Indeed, as the forces of liberalism were crushed so the controls over education and freedom of speech were increased with the establishment of the Institute for the Study of National Moral Culture in 1932 and the Bureau of Thought in 1934. In 1936 the Council for Renovating Education and Learning recommended the reform of school education along nationalistic lines so that much of the motivation in 1939 for making boys' attendance in youth schools compulsory up to the age of conscription at 19 was that young men would experience no break in their young lives from nationalistic propaganda and military training. When this vast programme of repression and propaganda came to a grinding halt in 1945 the question of what to replace it with lay with the Americans. Not unnaturally an American answer was given, first by MacArthur and his advisers and then most decisively by the United States Education Mission to Japan.

The work of the Mission as we have already seen, was brief and to the point but it set the seal of approval on MacArthur's early reforms and brought about a remarkable change in Japanese education. We shall examine four of the Mission's proposals that were the subject of specific action.

The first proposal concerned the abolition of the Imperial Rescript on Education and the quasi-religious ceremonies which surrounded it, together with the banning of obeisance before the imperial portrait. This brought to an end the practices of half a century in which the presence of the divine emperor in almost palpable form had penetrated to the heart and soul of every school in the country. The notion that the emperor was a man and not a god was a revolutionary concept for the Japanese people. Nevertheless, as they were permitted for the first time to gaze upon their emperor instead of bowing their heads down to the ground as he passed by, and as he, also for the first time, toured fields, hospitals and factories, it did indeed appear that he was a distinctively *human* middle-aged man, albeit a somewhat shy and bookish one. Indeed, his fate, like that of his people, was in the hands of the Americans, for soon after the surrender he had called on General MacArthur and declared that he should be held responsible for the war. MacArthur, at a personal level, was grieved 'to see a man once so high brought so low' (BBC, 1989); but, at a political level, he feared that Japan without an emperor might become ungovernable. As a result, on the grounds of expediency, the founder of the Showa era was granted a second opportunity, 20 years after his inauguration, to bring enlightened peace to his country, but the Imperial Rescript which had been revered as a sacred text for nearly 60 years was nullified by the National Diet in May 1948.

The second proposal, the dismantling of the differentiated pre-war system of secondary education and the expansion of compulsory schooling from six to nine years according to the American 6–3–3–4 model, posed great difficulties. These are summarized in the recollections of the then deputy minister for education, science and culture, as quoted by Okuda and Hishimura (1983, p. 569):

> The reform of the school system extending compulsory education to nine years and establishing the 6–3–3 system is comparable to the epoch-making school reforms of the Meiji period. In particular, the construction of schools needed after the devastation of the war and those needed for the future was, in terms of both quantity and speed, unprecedented in the entire history of Japan. The greater part of the burden of this construction was borne by local cities, towns and villages which had suffered heavy damage during the war. The pains and efforts of local officials in selecting and obtaining land, arranging to meet the necessary construction expenses, and completing it satisfactorily, defy words. Of course, the National Government made great efforts to respond to the demands of the people, but the poverty of the national treasury made it impossible to satisfy the needs of local cities, towns and villages. In spite of the lack of financial aid from the National Government, however, local people promoted the improvement of schools by donating land, clearing and leveling plots of land, and putting up with high taxes and demands for monetary contributions. During this period, there occurred many difficulties and sad

events which will go down as unprecedented in the history of education and administration, but the fruit of all these efforts was the construction of a large number of excellent schools.

The above quotation draws particular attention to the physical problems experienced by the Japanese in carrying out the recommendations of the Mission but there were equally demanding spiritual tests to be faced. It was one thing to carry out a heroic building programme in the face of appalling practical difficulties, but it was quite another to fill the vacuum created by the abolition of a document of the stature of the Imperial Rescript. The Japanese government feared that without the Rescript's presence in schools, teachers would lose their authority, students would lack discipline and the emperor, no longer divine, would lose all remaining respect.

The Americans understood very well the significance of the Rescript in underpinning pre-war totalitarianism, but suspected that the government in post-war Japan protested too much in asserting that the Rescript's call to loyalty and harmony actually supported democracy and not the misinterpretations drawn from it by the militarists. Therefore, the CIE instructed the Ministry of Education to produce a draft education law to replace the rescript. Meetings took place between CIE and the Ministry in November and December 1946 but there was much prevarication by the Japanese over the inclusion of specific references in the proposed new law to coeducation and democracy. In fact, there was considerable resistance to the notion of a clear and unambiguous document that ordinary people could understand. Nevertheless, the Fundamental Law of Education was enacted in March 1947 and replaced the Imperial Rescript in much the same way as the new constitution of October 1946 had replaced the Meiji constitution of 1889. Both aimed to uphold popular sovreignty and to sustain human rights and the former in particular sought to educate young people for democratic citizenship.

The third of the Mission's proposals, to help Japanese teachers form unions, was the easiest of all the proposals to realize since teachers were eager to unionize before the Mission had so much as begun its work. The Japan Teachers' Union (JTU) was founded on 1 December 1945 and the Japan Educators' Union (JEU) was established the following day. The two unions were soon at loggerheads. They became typecast as the left-wing or communist union (JTU) and the right-wing or reactionary union (JEU). It was the JTU which gained popular support. It sought to promote democracy in schools but also to gain a fivefold salary increase for teachers since the latter, in the face of rampant inflation, were existing on a mere pittance.

From the start GHQ encouraged the teachers' unions and the Ministry of Education, against its better judgement, was obliged to come round to this point of view. In a breast-beating document entitled *Guide to New Education in Japan* issued to teachers in 1946 and written in close collaboration with the CIE, the Ministry confessed to various shortcomings in the Japanese people, including a lack of critical spirit and a tendency to obey authority blindly. Later in 1947, in *A Tentative Suggested Course of Study*, there was a further confession that standardization and regimentation in schools had prevented the possibility of a lively and stimulating education. It says much for the central and authoritarian control of Japanese education that, in the case of the *Guide to New Education in Japan*, the Ministry felt obliged to state in the foreword that it was not necessary for teachers to memorize the book and teach it to their pupils as they would a textbook.

In all probability it was this very same heaviness of control over teachers by central government in the pre-war years that was the root cause of persistent conflict between the JTU and the Ministry of Education in succeeding post-war years. Certainly in 1945 relative power positions were dramatically reversed when left-wing groups emerged from the war (and often prison) with clean hands and the enthusiastic backing of GHQ while the Ministry of Education was forced to confess to past wrongs and submit all its output to rigorous examination by the CIE. But few, perhaps, would have forecast that public education would become the main arena for political conflict in the post-war period, particularly in a country renowned for harmony in industrial relationships. However, Rohlen (1983, p. 210), writing in this context, does not mince his words:

> The machinery of educational policy making has witnessed intense and persistent conflict between the Japan Teachers' Union (JTU) and government authorities, especially at the national level. Fist fights in the national legislature, teachers' strikes and sit-ins, mass arrests and legal suits have occurred regularly. Hostility, distrust and acrimony have often divided faculties and paralyzed schools.

Beauchamp (1987, p. 307), commenting a few years after Rohlen, confirms that 'relations between these two major educational forces have not improved significantly in recent years and prospects for real understanding and cooperation are not yet on the horizon', but he does quote a number of Japanese newspapers which suggest that 40 years after the founding of the JTU its membership has fallen to below 50 per cent of the teaching force for the first time. All in all, this state of affairs must rate as the strangest legacy of the United States Education Mission for in the 40 years since its departure it has taken all the considerable skills of local educational administrators to prevent conflicts between the two opposing bodies from affecting the education of the young in the classroom.

The fourth of the Mission's proposals, to institute local boards of education, was stillborn. The Board of Education Law, promulgated by the emperor in July 1948, failed signally to take root in Japanese soil. The proposal was that, after the American fashion, school boards be elected by popular vote in each community, from village to city, up and down the country. The boards were to be politically independent and were to exercise control over each primary and secondary school to which they were elected. By these means the Mission aimed to reduce the enormous powers of the Ministry of Education and to break down what they saw as an unwholesome willingness on the part of the Japanese people to obey the dictates of central government. In other words, it was hoped that by setting up new structures and procedures a new individualism would be released in Japanese citizens. The Americans expected active resistance to these measures from the Ministry of Education and in this they were not disappointed but, as with other reforming issues described above, the opposition was overcome. What was impossible to overcome, however, was the apathy of the general public. In an opinion poll of the day, a third of those interviewed knew nothing of the forthcoming board elections and, according to Kobayashi (1976 p. 46), the highest voting rate achieved in any community was 56 per cent. More seriously, the boards showed little desire to exercise any power, especially in curriculum matters; for example, the Ministry of Education's 'guide' to *Courses of Study* was treated, as it always had been, as a set of instructions. But power without resources is difficult to exercise and since the Ministry held whatever precious money was still available for education, it was a clear case of he who pays the piper calls the tune. The Board of Education Law did not long survive the departure of the Americans. In 1956 it was amended so that the popular vote was abolished and board members were appointed by prefectural governors or local mayors.

The work of the United States Education Mission had immediate effect. The raising of the school leaving age was achieved despite a shortage of resources, overcrowded classrooms and double or even triple shifts. New courses of study were prepared, textbooks printed and teaching reorientated, all under the watchful eye of the CIE. In April 1949 the Teachers' Certification Law required existing teachers to be retrained and entrants to the profession to take the equivalent of a four-year undergraduate course instead of the old two-year college course. Normal schools were reorganized and became either independent colleges of education or departments in the newly established state universities. On the surface, then, democratization was proceeding apace, but it may be doubted whether this was accompanied by major shifts in basic cultural values. Rohlen (1983, p. 69) thinks that in the area of his special interest — the high schools — 'the occupation's reforms were the least effective.'

In the United States the high school most commonly provides the last three years' education in the 6–3–3 system, although some areas still retain the 8–4 system. The high school is characterized by open admission to local residents, coeducation and a mix of academic, vocational and general courses. In addition, individualism in dress and study programmes is encouraged in order to prepare students to play a full part as citizens of their local community. In the immediate post-war years, however, circumstances were not propitious for transplanting the ideal American high school into the Japanese educational system. The Fundamental Law of Education (1947) extended compulsory full-time education from six to nine years, so that scarce resources were stretched to the limit to provide places at the newly designated middle schools. However, these new middle schools were in reality the old upper elementary schools which had provided most of the population with two years' education after the compulsory elementary school so that in practice new provision was required for only one extra school year. But when the graduates of the new middle schools turned in increasing numbers to the newly designated high schools (the pre-war ordinary middle schools) there was quite simply not enough room for all to attend. Since open admission to local residents was out of the question, the entrance examination was retained by both local government and private schools as a well-tried method of dealing with excess demand for high school education. Consequently, study programmes were not greatly changed and few teachers changed jobs. Indeed, the only significant development was that the girls' high schools disappeared overnight to be replaced by equality of educational opportunity at the secondary level. Otherwise competition to enter the academic high schools remained severe and the old distinction between academic and vocational schools was preserved. Thus, in the late 1940s the distinctively Japanese pattern of high school education was laid down and the American model of high school education was lost to view. It is true, of course, that when the occupation came to an end, many new high schools were built but the majority were either academic *or* vocational, rather than comprehensive. It is equally true that attendance levels at high schools rose to over 90 per cent, but in every school district in the country high schools were vertically ranked and reflected not social and academic diversity but social and academic segregation and stratification.

If the Japanese high schools symbolize the endurance of key educational values in the face of the recommendations of the American Mission then the education of the present emperor, Akihito, can be seen as a metaphor for the rapid progress of Japan towards economic and national independence during the seven years of American occupation. In 1946 the Emperor Hirohito entertained members of the Mission at the Imperial Palace and asked the chairman to find an

American tutor for his 12-year-old son. Eventually a tutor was selected who taught the crown prince until he was 15 years old, whereupon there were suggestions that he continue his education at an American school and an English university. In the event, however, he attended a private university at Gakushuin in Tokyo, famous in pre-war years for the presence of the sons of the nobility within its elite gates. Clearly, as the occupation neared its end the imperial household felt that the necessity for the young prince to embrace the language and culture of the English-speaking world had lessened while the need for the future emperor to support the rehabilitation of his own people had increased. But there were also doubts in the United States concerning the reception the young prince might receive there so soon after the end of the Pacific War.

One final proof, if proof be needed, the basic cultural values in Japan were not dislocated by the recommendations of the Mission is found in the fate that befell the suggestion by two minority writers of the Mission's report that the Japanese script be romanized. In fact Japan's first education minister, Mori Arinori, had suggested in the Meiji period that the English language should replace the Japanese because the former gave better expression to the new science and technology than the latter could ever do, and ironically it was Mori's American adviser of the time, David Murray, who counselled strongly against this notion. But it seems that no one advised George Counts and Robert Hall in 1946 to drop their attempt to persuade the Japanese to render their language in the letters of the English alphabet. Extensive experiments in the schools were carried out, but by the end of 1950 the CIE was convinced that without a major revision of the Japanese vocabulary this reform could never be realized. In any case the English language *per se* was more popular with the Japanese people than ever before despite or perhaps because of the fact that the reforming zeal of the Americans had peaked and the first stage of the occupation was over.

As early as 1947 MacArthur had felt that the time had come for the ending of the occupation but it was not possible to persuade the Allies of this until 1951. A number of factors, however, concentrated American thinking. First, the cost of getting Japan on its feet was proving enormous, with the bill for 1947 alone exceeding $400 million (Storry, 1976, p. 253). Second, the advent of the Korean war in 1950 made it imperative that Japan was politically stable so that nearly all the troops of occupation could be withdrawn. Third, the United Nations forces in Korea needed a thriving Japanese economy to keep them supplied. In fact, it was the Korean war that brought about an economic boom in Japan reminiscent of the prosperity enjoyed by the Japanese when supplying the Allies during the First World War. Finally, the San Francisco Peace Treaty of 28 April 1952, which placed no limitation on the freedom of Japan to trade, set the stage for the most remarkable economic phoenix ever to rise from the ashes of a war-devastated country. Equally, from the ruins of bombed and broken schools arose a system that supplied the economy with perhaps the best-educated workforce in the world. It is to the development of this educational system that we now turn.

The school system, 1953–1987

A number of post-war educational reforms have lasted until the present time. These include the institution of the 6–3–3 grade structure on the lines of the American model, the introduction of coeducation into junior and senior high schools and the encouragement of equal opportunity at all levels of school education. Other reforms to do with the writing system and the school boards were quickly abandoned or modified after the restoration of national sovereignty in 1952. However, moral education, which was abolished by the Americans, was reintroduced in 1958, though without the nationalistic overtones characteristic of pre-war thought control. The legal basis of contemporary Japanese education is enshrined in the Fundamental Law of Education and the School Education Law, both of 1947. The aim of both laws is to create moral and capable citizens by means of free, compulsory coeducation of nine years' duration, from ages 6 to 15, at elementary and lower secondary or junior high schools. However, from the beginning of our period most Japanese children experienced some form of pre-elementary education before the age of six.

Pre-elementary education

A consideration of the important part played by the home and family, especially that of the mother, in the education of Japanese children will be held over until the next chapter because our present purpose is limited to a description of the educational system. Pre-elementary education in Japan is not compulsory nor is it linked to elementary education, but it is strongly supported by almost all parents. Children attend either kindergarten (*yochien*) between three and five years of age or nursery schools (*hoikuen*) which accept children from infancy. The former operate under the aegis of the Ministry of Education and the latter are established by the Ministry of Welfare. The combined attendance levels at both types of institution range from 40 per cent of three-year-olds to over 90 per cent of all four- and five-year-olds (Leestma *et al.*, 1987, p. 79). The kindergartens are open for about five hours a day, while the day nurseries, which are primarily for the children of working mothers, are in session for around eight hours.

The state provides about a quarter of the institutions and makes a modest subsidy available to the private pre-elementary schools. Tuition fees are charged but at the nursery schools these vary according to the level of parental income. The schools are generally staffed by young qualified teachers who have studied child psychology, physical education, music and the arts. Classes are large, with about 30 pupils to one teacher, so that the child is introduced as early as possible, after the rather self-centred experience of home, to the idea of group needs and responsibilities. Lively and boisterous activity is encouraged, indeed it is *de rigueur*, and those children who do not join in may be ostracized by both teacher and class and treated as if their behaviour were strange or peculiar (*okashii*) (Hendry, 1986, p. 144).

The official guidelines for pre-elementary education stress the importance of developing the health of infants, both physical and mental, and giving them experience of language, music and crafts. Consequently children are encouraged to express themselves freely but correctly in speech, to sing and play simple musical instruments and to work at paper-folding (*origami*). However, pressure from parents on the pre-elementary schools to introduce their children to basic reading and writing skills is on the increase and in a situation where most of the schools are open to market forces it is likely that in order to remain competitive they will develop in line with the consumers' declared interests.

In Britain a recent report by the House of Commons Education, Science and Arts Committee (1988) estimated that only 44 per cent of three- and four-year-olds experience any form of pre-school education. This situation exists despite a White Paper entitled *Education: A Framework for Expansion* (DES, 1972), issued by Margaret Thatcher when she was Secretary of State for Education, which recommended nursery education for 50 per cent of three-year-olds and 90 per cent of four-year-olds before 1982. In fact in 1988 *ad hoc* playgroups offered the majority of pre-school places but their contribution is of a varied and diverse kind and is practically never available to children on a daily basis. Nursery provision in Britain is limited and almost equalled by places for under fives in primary schools but neither provision is available to all parents who would like it for their children. The recommendations of the committee make clear just how far Britain is behind Japan in the first step on the educational ladder. For example, little is known about the actual demand for pre-school education; places for initial and in-service training for early-years teachers are insufficient; and finally, a framework for the qualifications of teachers in the under-fives sector does not exist and is urgently required.

Interestingly an OECD (1971, p. 59) report on Japanese education concluded that it was difficult to find any studies which actually confirm the widely held supposition that kindergarten education is beneficial to children in terms of later scholastic ability. The House of Commons report cited above found, similarly, that there was no conclusive proof that nursery education had long-lasting effects. Nevertheless, in the absence of proof the Japanese people and government have backed the hunch that positive benefits for pre-school education exist even if they slip through the net of scientific enquiries. In Britain, nearly 20 years after *Education: A Framework for Expansion*, it is possible that in the 1990s its modest aims will once again be pursued.

For those readers interested in the day-to-day activity of pre-elementary schools in Japan as seen through the eyes of a Western visitor, Hendry's (1986) text is indispensable. Much of her experience centred round the private kindergarten her son attended for six months in 1981 in Tateyama City in Chiba prefecture and which by her own admission was somewhat unusual in that it attracted particularly the children of wealthy and ambitious parents. The head-mistress, who had spent some years in California and who offered English as a speciality, strove for high levels of excellence and discipline. Her staff, for example, frequently worked a 12-hour day, six days a week, and were 'advised' by her in matters of dress and manners. However, Hendry also visited large city-centre public kindergartens with about 900 pupils apiece as well as small rural kindergartens with 100 children. The rural schools were not only smaller than the rest but were also more relaxed since the parents of the pupils were by and large less well off and less ambitious. Nursery schools were also plentiful in Tateyama. One establishment took infants from as young as three months as well as caring for elementary school children whose parents were still at work at the end of the school day. Indeed, part of the rationale for day nurseries in Japan is to allow parents both to work, if this is demanded by their economic circumstances, and to have time to develop their social and cultural lives together. However, as we shall see in the next chapter, there is strong social pressure on mothers in Japan not to work but to stay at home and look after the children.

Elementary education (grades 1–6)

State elementary or primary school (*shogakko*) is where, at the age of six, nearly all Japanese children begin their first nine years' compulsory education. Private education at this level is rare and is found only in large cities, where less than 1 per cent of the nation's most precocious children enter fee-paying schools. Thus, in the community at large starting at the local school is a major event in a child's life which is treated on all sides as a solemn rite of passage. At home many children are presented with a desk and chair as well as presents and congratulations. At school they attend, along with their mothers, a formal ceremony in which senior pupils, school officials and local dignitaries welcome them into the learning society. The school buildings themselves are never grand; rather they are plain, functional and always scrupulously clean. Surprising as it may seem to Western visitors, it is the children who clean the schools as part of their daily programme. The purpose of the exercise is not to save money but to develop character and, to judge by the high levels of cleanliness on every side in Japan, this policy succeeds handsomely. Richard Gordon Smith, an early twentieth-century English traveller in Japan, noticed the custom in 1905 and thought it an excellent idea but one which required discipline 'of an almost military kind' (Manthorpe, 1986, p. 189). If Smith had in mind an authoritarian and hierarchical army-style discipline, however, then he was far from the truth.

In Japan elementary school classes are large by Western standards, around 35 students on average, yet the children are well behaved and attentive and spend up to a third more time on their tasks than do comparable American students (Leestma *et al*, 1987, p. 27). This state of affairs is not achieved by authoritarian teaching methods but by the delegation of management powers and responsibilities by teachers to mixed ability groups (*han*) of four to six children. In Japanese schools *han* are the primary work groups for activities that include academic projects, discipline procedures and cleaning chores. Thus all students are given the opportunity to experience leadership roles and to understand how small-group processes work in the pursuit of common goals. In the more senior classes in elementary school some students, who are the elected representatives of their class, experience real decision-making at the level of school government. In fact, Japanese children are encouraged from their earliest years to take considerable responsibility for their own behaviour and learning as well as that of the *han* to which they belong. The corollary of this is that teachers in Japan are more able than their colleagues in many Western countries to concentrate on teaching because matters of class control and organization are taken care of by the children themselves.

The curriculum in elementary schools in Japan is tightly controlled by the Ministry of Education (*Monbusho*) and, for each subject and grade, course content is closely prescribed. Only textbooks with the imprimatur of *Monbusho* can be used, although teachers may include supplementary material in their lessons if they wish. However, the textbooks are given to the children free of charge and become their personal property.

The most immediate task to face elementary school children, and on which they spend about a quarter of their time, is learning how to read and write their own language. For reasons discussed in Chapter 1, the Japanese script is a combination of Chinese characters and

Japanese phonetic symbols. Thus children have to master two Japanese syllabaries of 41 symbols each, *hiragana* for Japanese words and *katakana* for foreign words. In addition, they have to learn about two thousand Chinese symbolic characters, *kanji*, which are visually more complex than the characters of the Japanese syllabaries. The Japanese syllabaries are learnt in the first grade, along with 76 Chinese characters, but by the time compulsory school is completed nine years later it is expected that pupils will have mastered all the Chinese characters and achieved basic literacy. However, the task of reading is further complicated by the fact that sometimes the texts are read Western style (horizontally from left to right) as in arithmetic and science lessons, and sometimes in traditional Japanese style (vertically from top to bottom and right to left) as in language lessons. Furthermore, individual words are not separated in the text but have to be identified by the context and, to cap it all, Chinese characters present problems of pronunciation. The Chinese themselves employ different tones to signify different meanings attached to identical characters, but the Japanese, who employ no variation of tone to differentiate meaning, are faced with many ambiguities. Not surprisingly, Stevenson *et al.* (1986, p. 232) found that 'Japanese children are not as fluent in reading *kanji* as Chinese children'. However, the main thrust of this research was to compare the reading ability of Japanese and American elementary school children, and here it was found, contrary to some expectations, that Japanese children performed no more effectively than their American counterparts. Indeed, on both sides of the Pacific severe reading problems were experienced.

The Japanese are the first to acknowledge that some children experience great difficulties with their studies and that schools with large classes and detailed programmes of work are not best suited to deal with those who fall behind, nevertheless, it is in Japan uniquely that parents pick up the problem of remedial education. Indeed, it is the readiness of Japanese parents to pay for enrichment programmes for their children that has led to the growth of a vast network of private profit-making *juku* or cram schools which run parallel with the formal educational system. A more detailed treatment of *juku* will be given later in this chapter; here it is sufficient to note that nearly one-third of all sixth grade (or 11-year-old) children attend *juku* and that the two subjects most commonly studied are arithmetic and the Japanese language.

Learning to write in Japanese commences in the third grade when children are eight, and follows the traditional methods handed down from the Tokugawa era: consequently brushes and ink are still used in order to master the gentle art of calligraphy. Arithmetic begins in the first grade and is second only to the Japanese language in the amount of time devoted to it throughout elementary school. Japanese language is timetabled for eight periods a week in the first four grades and six in the fifth and sixth, whereas arithmetic is allocated four periods in the first grade and five thereafter. A period lasts 45 minutes. As with language so with mathematics: *juku* assists many pupils in keeping up with a tough school programme which introduces new mathematical concepts and skills grade by grade with little time for repetition and review. Nevertheless in international tests of achievement in mathematics Japanese children consistently outperform others.

Stigler *et al.* (1982) reported on the mathematical ability of Japanese and American elementary school children at six and ten years of age as part of the same major comparative study cited above. Unlike the tests of reading ability, however, where the results in both countries were broadly comparable, the tests of mathematical ability yielded highly significant differences, indicating that first at six years of age and even more at ten years the Japanese sample outperformed its American counterpart. Considerable care was taken in this study to select comparable samples and to administer fair tests, so it is difficult to escape from the conclusion that Japanese children's abilities in mathematics are outstanding in their first year or grade of primary education and that they appreciate thereafter more rapidly than those of their American peers.

Science is also a subject where Japanese children show superiority. This subject is studied for two periods a week in the first two years of elementary school and three periods a week for the remaining four years with the aim that, by sixth grade, children are thoroughly versed in the basic elements of the scientific method and can, therefore, design and carry out simple experiments and document their observations and results. Comber and Keeves (1973) studied scientific achievement in 18 countries and found that Japanese ten-years-olds obtained the highest average scores of any nation in tests that covered physics, biology, chemistry and earth sciences. Thus the mean or average score for the Japanese sample was 21.7, the United States 17.7 and England 15.7. It is noteworthy that the Japanese scored well on tests of both factual knowledge and the application of scientific principles.

Outside the three core subjects of language, arithmetic and science Japanese children study in six other areas which may for convenience be seen as two groups of three subjects each. The first group, social studies, moral education and homemaking is intended to enhance the child's understanding of the cultural values of his society in the broadest sense. Social studies, the most academic of the three, looks at society from the micro to the macro level and stresses the relatedness of the different levels and the child's responsibilities to that society. Moral education, the most personal of the three, seeks to inculcate the highest possible standards in personal and social life. It occupies one period a week in the timetable but is far from being 'bolted on', for its subject matter suffuses school life and thus the class period becomes a focus for and reinforcement of school values. Home-making, the most practical of the three, occurs in the last two years of elementary school. Its content includes cooking and sewing but, as its title indicates, the basic aim is to give children a practical under-standing of family life and the skills necessary to make a contribution to that life. The second group of subjects, music, arts and craft and physical education, has more to do with cultural values in the narrow sense. The music syllabus is broad and includes singing, the playing of simple instruments and the appreciation of Western and Japanese music. Arts and craft is also wide-ranging, from drawing and painting through print-making to sculpture. Finally, physical education is intended to lead to a life-long enjoyment of sport and health related exercise. The syllabus includes athletics, sport, gymnastics and dance as well as swimming, usually in the school pool, and ice skating in winter on a specially flooded rink in the school grounds.

As we have noted above, the tradition in Japan is for the curriculum to be tightly controlled by *Monbusho*. By contrast, for most of the twentieth century but particularly for the period between the Education Acts of 1944 and 1988, the tradition in England and Wales has favoured local control of the curriculum with considerable teacher autonomy. However, the Education Reform Act of 1988 consciously brought this tradition to an end by enhancing the powers of the Secretary of State for Education, Kenneth Baker at the time of the passing of the Act, increasing the executive strength of the Depart-ment of Education and Science (DES) and imposing a national curricu-lum and system of assessment on all public sector or 'maintained' primary and secondary schools. Shortly after the Act was passed, the DES published proposals for appropriate attainment targets and pro-grammes of study in the three core subjects English, science and mathematics.

The authors of *Mathematics for ages 5 to 16* (DES, 1988a, p. 5) were very much aware that they were 'breaking new ground in attempting to develop a mathematics curriculum with continuity and progression through from primary reception class to the secondary fifth form'. It was appropriate, therefore, that they should visit a country like Japan which possessed considerable experience of such a curriculum. Also, as part of the process of informing their work, it was decided that the members of the working group should make study visits to three countries that had taken part in an, as yet unpublished, international study of pupil performance in mathematics. The members, however, were privy to the results of the study and knew that Japanese students had achieved significantly higher scores than pupils in 19 other countries. A visit to Japan was thus strongly suggested on two counts.

The authors admit, however, that in advance of their visit they 'suspected' that superior performance in mathematics would be due as much to 'cultural and sociological differences as to the efficiency of Japanese provision in mathematics education' (DES, 1988a, p. 112). In their eight-day visit the members of the working group became convinced that their 'suspicions' were well grounded. Consequently, they ascribe the success of mathematics education in Japan to respect for the subject, respect for teachers, an unparalelled work ethic and the fact that mathematics is a *sine qua non* for university entrance. The work ethic, in conjunction with fear of failure, was seen as the explanation for the heroic endeavours of below-average pupils.

Members of the working party observed several lively and interesting mathematics lessons in schools but believed them to be the exception rather than the rule; they also witnessed some impersonal and tedious *juku* classes which they appeared to take for the norm. Nevertheless, they concluded that achievement in mathematics in schools in Japan *is* higher than in the UK, that pupils are more highly motivated and teachers more greatly respected. Significantly, there are no teacher shortages in Japan. They felt that in Britain expectations of what pupils can achieve need to be raised and that the government, if it means business, must seriously address the question of how to maintain 'an adequately manned [and] well motivated teacher force' (DES, 1988a, p. 118).

The teachers in Japanese elementary schools spend just over 20 hours a week inside the classroom but much time outside in preparation and planning. About 60 per cent of class teachers are women, but 98 per cent of the principals are men. Teachers enjoy a six-week summer vacation, which is long by Japanese standards, but they use this time to update their skills and knowledge and supervise vacation activities and projects for their pupils. Lewis (1988, p. 160) found that in Tokyo regulations limited the length of time that an individual teacher could spend in any one school and she conjectured that the rotation of teachers around schools ensured greater uniformity in the elementary sector in Tokyo than would be the case in a major metropolitan area in the United States.

For those readers interested in one Western researcher's view of a day in the life of 15 Tokyo first-grade classrooms, Lewis's (1988) article is recommended. She observed at first hand the way six-year-old monitors, on a rota basis, learned how to share authority for classroom management with their teacher; she saw how teachers refrained from intervening in small mixed-ability *han* when children were experiencing peer pressures and sanctions; and she noted that group and self-criticism were encouraged as a spur to greater effort, but that the overall aim of first-grade teachers was for their charges to feel relaxed and emotionally stable at school. It seems, therefore, that at elementary school Japanese children are initiated early into organizing and being responsible for their own learning, working amicably and productively as members of a group, as well as practising self-discipline and developing good study habits. Certainly they need all these qualities to sustain them as they progress up the educational ladder.

Lower secondary or junior high school education
(grades 7–9)

The transition from elementary school (*shogakko*) to lower secondary school (*chugakko*) is a second important rite of passage in the life of the young Japanese. Two ceremonies mark the occasion: first, the graduation from elementary school of a *jido* (child); and second, the initiation into middle school of a *seito* (student). As a *jido* at elementary school, the pupil was addressed by his or her first name with a suffix (*chan*) indicating juvenile status, but as a *seito* at the lower secondary school, sometimes called middle school, he or she will be called by the family name with a suffix, *kun* for a boy or *san* for a girl indicating an increase in formality in relationships. The two ceremonies are but two weeks apart: the first towards the end of March and the second in early April as the cherry trees come into blossom, an obvious but beautiful symbol of new life. Another outward sign of a new beginning is the distinctive uniforms that middle school students adopt. There is no official national policy on school uniforms but foreign visitors could be forgiven for thinking otherwise, since on all school visits to national and religious centres, such as those at Nara and Kyoto, parties of junior high school students assemble in well-behaved groups with each school identified by boys in military-style high-collared jackets and black trousers and girls in navy blue sailor suits.

These uniforms are seen at their brightest and best at the lower secondary school initiation ceremony when approximately 94 per cent of local 12-year-olds gather, with their parents and relatives, to mark the beginning of their secondary education and of their last three years' compulsory education. These lower secondary schools are the same institutions that came into being as a direct result of the recommendation of the United States Education Mission to Japan in 1947 and they are in most respects schools for the local community, except that approximately 3 per cent of the relevant age group attend private establishments. Like elementary schools, the junior high school buildings are functional and simple in design, with classrooms that are bare apart from neat rows of chairs and desks. Notices on the walls are few and far between, with the notable exception of the classroom cleaning schedule. Cleaning is organized by the students and is not the responsibility of the teachers or of ancillary staff. Teams of cleaners, which are so much a part of the English education system, simply do not exist in Japan although, of course, maintenance staff are employed. Perhaps even more surprising, in a country synonymous with high technology, is the absence of computers and other technical teaching aids. For example, the writers of *Mathematics for ages 5 to 16* (DES, 1988a, p. 116) were told that only 18 per cent of junior high schools possessed computers and that the average number per school was three. The same authors also report that they found practically no evidence for the use of calculators in Japanese schools, at the same time, however, they made no reference to the widespread use of the abacus in Japan.

The abacus (*soroban*) has been popular in Japan for over three hundred years and is used widely as an aid to calculating. Most commonly, the *soroban* measures about 30 cm by 5 cm and has a wooden frame holding 21 rods containing five sliding beads each with one above a horizontal beam and four below. A decimal system is used with a unit point at every third rod. The *soroban* is durable and costs about £10. In most everyday calculations like addition and subtraction it is quicker than a calculator. A Loughborough student of education and mathematics attended a *juku soroban* session in 1988 and was astonished at the speed at which pupils operated. For example, one 11-year-old girl worked a long division sum with a dividend of eight digits and a divisor of four in 14 seconds. The use of the abacus, therefore, by reason of its speed, accuracy and convenience, forms 'part of the curriculum in all grade schools as one of the elements of arithmetic' (Lambert, 1989, pp. 31–43).

After the initiation ceremony into middle school comes the introduction to intensive formal academic study that will climax in the third year or ninth grade with senior high school entrance examinations. To this end, most lessons will take the form of lectures with students copying from the blackboard into notebooks. Each lecture will last for a full 50 minutes. The textbooks, approved by *Monbusho*, will be the basis of most lessons and will be followed closely by teachers and pupils alike, but teachers will additionally work from a manual to which they will adhere with varying degrees of closeness according to their individual interests and abilities. At worst, important points will be copied slavishly from the manual to the blackboard and thence to the notebook, with the child being treated as little more than a cipher; but at best, as the author observed in 1987, young, enthusiastic teachers will gain a lively response from large, well-behaved and interested classes.

In order to give their lectures the teachers attend the room where the students are based. This room, known as the homeroom (*homurumu*), also has one teacher assigned to it to act as an adviser or counsellor. Typically, a brief homeroom meeting takes place every day before lessons begin, but once a week a full period of 50 minutes' duration is set aside for the discussion of personal or school affairs. I witnessed one such homeroom period in April 1987 during which the teacher sat at the back of the class and took no obvious part in the proceedings. At the front two students were organizing the sleeping arrangements for a forthcoming school trip. They had drawn a plan on the board of the available accommodation and they were chairing a lively discussion on the allocation of people to rooms. This was not, perhaps, a profound experience of democracy in practice, in line with the intentions of the Americans in introducing this particular period into Japanese schools; nevertheless, it was impressive to see a large group of young adolescents working constructively on an administrative matter which was, to them, of some importance. However, the subject of most importance for most students at lower secondary school is the examinations that control entrance to upper secondary education. Consequently, the prime task of the counsellor is to give his or her students the best possible advice on which upper school examination to attempt. This advice depends crucially on each student's ability to get to grips with the junior high school curriculum.

The individual subjects of the secondary school curriculum are mostly familiar to students who have recently left elementary school. The study of Japanese language, for example, is continued in middle school until students have been introduced to all the two thousand Chinese characters necessary for basic literacy in Japanese but students will also attempt to read for the first time short passages from the Chinese classics in the archaic language that dominated the education of the *samurai* in the Tokugawa period. It is almost as if all British students in comprehensive schools were to be introduced to some of the finer passages from *Beowulf* in the original Old English. In social studies, the history and geography learned at elementary school is developed and students are introduced to civics and economics. Much emphasis is placed on the pupils' ability to use and interpret the tools of the trade of social studies such as maps, tables and statistics. The students' ability to present the results of observations and surveys in report form is also considered important. In mathematics, the study of arithmetical concepts is rounded off and students are introduced to algebra, geometry, probability and statistics. As we have already noted, it is not difficult to find evidence that Japanese students lead the world in their attainment in mathematics.

Prais (1986, p. 124) draws attention to the results of two impeccably organized international comparisons of mathematical achievement in 1964 and 1981. In 1964, 70 agreed questions in mathematics were put to large representative samples of pupils in a dozen countries. In

England 3,200 pupils gained an average correct score of 19.3 (out of 70) and in Japan 2,050 pupils obtained an average of 31.2. The average age of the pupils in both countries was 13.5 years. Interestingly, England was well represented among students who obtained the highest scores (over 61), being second only to Japan; but England also had the dubious distinction of being better represented among the lowest scores (below 5) than any other nation. The 1981 survey revealed that the relative positions of England and Japan had changed little in the intervening 17 years, except that the Japanese position had improved slightly and the English worsened.

Results of this sort from international surveys are variously interpreted. Lynn (1988, p. 17) concludes that 'the average Japanese twelve year old is approximately at the same academic level as the average fifteen year old in the West'. Leestma *et al.* (1987, p. 35) draw attention to the view that the normal pace of all Japanese students in mathematics, and most other subjects, at lower secondary level is equivalent to 'the fast track in a good suburban school system in the US'. Prais (1986) underlines the singular success of the Japanese education system with the average pupil and fears that Western economists have not really grasped the point that it is the 'typical pupil who goes on to become a typical member of the work force'. We shall return to Prais's argument when considering vocational education below.

The study of science at lower secondary school continues in biology, physics and chemistry and, according to the international study of scientific achievement by Comber and Keeves (1973) which was cited above with respect to ten-year-olds, Japanese 14-year-olds achieve the highest average scores (31.2) with the Americans at 21.6 and the English at 21.3. However, it cannot be said that at junior high schools other subjects are neglected in the pursuit of excellence in mathematics and science. For example in music and the fine arts a full programme of two 50 minute periods each per week is maintained until the final examination year, when the time allocation is halved. In health and physical education, by contrast, three periods each week are used throughout the full three years to encourage participation in individual and team sports. In addition, boys are introduced to traditional martial arts like judo and girls to expressive dance. In industrial arts/homemaking the sexes are free to choose their area but in practice most boys opt for experience in wood, metal, engine maintenance and electrical circuitry, and girls for cooking, dressmaking and child care. For the first time, at lower secondary school, an elective in language is introduced, but in practice, at most schools, the only language available is English. This amounts to a formal study of reading and writing in English with oral work kept to a minimum, partly because the university entrance examinations contain no oral element but also because the expertise of the teachers in idiomatic spoken English is usually limited. Duke (1986, p. xx) observes that 'foreign language instruction has improved the least in Japanese schools during the last forty years'. Finally, moral education continues throughout middle school with the aim of developing the students' characters to the highest level. Certainly self-control, a popular theme in these lessons, is required as students head towards their first experience of *juken jigoku* or 'examination hell'.

Juken jigoku comes about because of the nearly universal desire in Japan to continue in full-time education beyond the school leaving age of 15. To this end, nearly all ninth-grade students take at least one 14-plus examination in order to enter a local upper secondary school. The roots of this entrance examination lie, as we have seen, in the competition in the pre-war years to enter ordinary and higher middle schools and in the post-war years to attend the newly designated upper secondary schools. In both areas demand exceeded supply, but even when sufficient places became available they were not perceived as equally attractive. In fact, as Rohlen (1983, p. 121), the doyen of Western writers on Japanese secondary education, has observed, 'the ranking of high schools in a given locality is as clear — if not clearer — to all citizens as is the ranking of universities on a national scale'. The main criterion has for many years been the age of the school: thus the institutions that were originally the pre-war middle schools are seen as the best and the newly-built high schools are perceived as the least desirable. However, the least desired of all are without doubt the night high schools because they are evening institutes for the tiny minority (less than 2 per cent in 1984) who have been obliged to leave school at 15 but who still wish to obtain a high school diploma. Very often the ranking of high schools remains unchanged from year to year because the 'best' schools attract the 'best' candidates and consequently local prophecies fulfil themselves. Generally speaking, the most lowly ranked public (or state-maintained) high schools are preferred to the private or independent schools since the latter tend to be filled with those who have failed to gain entry to the former. However, increasingly there are some exceptions to this rule; Nada private school in Kobe, to be described later, is one. The least desirable institutions of all, apart from the night high schools, are the vocational high schools and the worst private schools. The vocational schools do not enjoy parity of esteem with the academic secondary schools because students who go to the former have failed entrance examinations to the latter and are the children of parents who cannot afford to send them to private school. In addition, the worst private schools suffer from delinquency problems and are ranked in the public mind below even the vocational schools, except that even the least desirable private schools offer college preparatory courses which, in a country where about one-third of the population presently aspire to higher education, is not an inconsiderable attraction.

In England, where nearly 70 per cent of 16-year-olds leave school at the end of their compulsory full-time education, comprehensive schools devote much time to arranging work experience and giving career guidance; but in Japan, where less than 10 per cent of 15-year-olds leave school at the end of their compulsory education, the junior high schools play a major role in placing students in the upper secondary school which offers an education most commensurate with their ability. Singleton (1967, pp. 37–40) describes the process as it operated in one prefecture over 20 years ago but it is clear from more recent reports that the essentials have changed little in the intervening period. For example, in the second year of middle school, practice tests are taken by the vast majority of students in the prefecture 'so that teachers and children can see how each individual compares with the prefectural norms and distribution'. These tests do not emanate from the prefectural education office but from private educational enterprises which flourish on all sides in Japan. Nevertheless, they enable the schools to build up a picture of their pupils' abilities and they give the pupils preparation and practice for the real thing. In truth, the children at Nichu middle school, where Singleton carried out his study, were not lacking in practice since 'the real thing' was the twenty-seventh test that they had taken in their third and final year! However, across the country similar batteries of tests yield such a plethora of data that a remarkably accurate match is achieved between those students leaving compulsory, homogeneous and undifferentiated middle schools and those entering non-compulsory, heterogeneous and differentiated high schools. In other words, by a process of guidance, counselling and tests the transfer of students from junior high to senior high school is achieved with a good fit between the numbers of applicants and the number of places available. The role of the teachers in the success of this operation appears to be crucial but is surprisingly underrecorded in the literature. However, the teachers appear to devote most of their energy to placing academic pupils in the public high schools and rather less energy to those students seeking entry to private, vocational and night schools.

Singleton (1967) found that teachers, in the absence of formal channels of information about the precise levels of achievement required to gain entry to individual high schools, set up their own information-gathering organization. Since each individual middle school receives information from the local high schools about the previous year's entrance examination results, it is possible for the local middle schools to pool their knowledge and to gain a fairly accurate picture of the minimum number of points required in the prefectural entrance examination of a particular high school. However, this information is not definitive since the number of pupils and their individual abilities fluctuate from year to year. Furthermore, since so much hangs on the examination results for both middle schools and their pupils, Singleton found that the deliberate feeding of misinformation into the equation could not be ruled out as a possible ploy by an individual school in order to gain an advantage.

Rohlen (1983, p. 126), writing some 16 years after Singleton, describes the system in Hyogo prefecture, approximately 250 miles west of Tokyo, where the four public academic high schools rely to a very considerable extent on the recommendation of the middle school teachers to fill their places. The students do not thereby escape the treadmill of the many preparatory tests which culminate in the entrance examination but they are directed specifically to apply to the school which the teachers think is the right one for them. Leestma *et al.* (1987, p. 38) confirm this general picture, except that they note a new tendency whereby the most able students may be accepted at high school on the recommendation of the middle school alone, without being subjected to the pressure of the entrance examination. If this tendency were to become more generalized then what the Japanese themselves regard as one of the worst aspects of their educational system might be removed or at least mitigated.

The senior high school entrance examination therefore constitutes an intense rite of passage for 14-year-old junior high school students and is frequently held responsible for what is described by Japanese writers as a 'crisis' in the education system (Nishimura, 1985). There are a number of strands which contribute to this perceived crisis. First, because of a centrally controlled curriculum, Japanese compulsory education is delivered with remarkable uniformity throughout the country to classes that are neither streamed nor tracked. Second, promotion from grade to grade is automatic and differential achievement by pupils is invariably ascribed to differences in effort expended rather than to differences in ability. Third, state schools provide little in the way of remedial education and so those who cannot keep up with the ever advancing school curriculum or who fear that the teaching they receive is not sufficient for their needs turn to *juku* for extra tuition and examination preparation. Thus it is estimated that nationwide about 50 per cent of final year junior high school students attend *juku* for about five hours a week, most commonly to enhance their performance in English and mathematics. Doubtless the majority of Japanese young people cope well with the pressures of one of the most demanding educational systems in the world, but a minority of lower secondary school students seek a more violent outlet for their difficulties and frustrations caused by the remorseless progress of the school curriculum.

Japan is presently a country where violence is abhorred. Western war veterans may find this statement difficult to accept but the fact remains that visitors to Japan feel safe at any time of day or night in any large city and, as Smith (1983, p. 124) has shown, the balance in the control of violent crime between Tokyo and New York City is heavily in favour of the former. Hence the occurrence of violent behaviour in schools, especially in lower secondary schools, causes sensational reports to appear in the national press. In the mid-1980s the number of violent incidents did decline but nevertheless, just over 10 per cent of lower secondary schools witnessed some form of school violence. According to Reeves (1985, p. 24), the peak year for incidents was 1982, when 1,123 junior high school teachers were attacked, compared with only 39 senior high school teachers. Japanese writers are aware that the incidence of violence in schools in their country seems remarkably low to Western observers, yet they still find present levels extremely worrying and regard them as one of the foremost reasons for bringing about educational reform (Ikuo, 1986, p. 2). Bullying (*ijime*) is also seen as a disturbing feature of Japanese school life, particularly as 80 per cent of reported cases occur in lower secondary schools (White, 1987, p. 138). Curiously, explanations of bullying in Japan often dwell on the personalities of the bullied rather than the bullies themselves because in a country where uniformity and conformity are highly valued, students that are slow, quiet or secretive stand out from the group and appear to become victims of their own marginality.

But it is suicide which is commonly cited by Western observers as the most unpleasant result of excessive pressure on the young in Japanese schools. However, the evidence to support this proposition is not easily found. Rohlen (1983, p. 328) makes the point that 'the juvenile suicide rate was dropping rapidly at the same time as matriculation rates to Japanese high schools and universities were rising'. While the proportion of 15–17-year-olds enrolled in high schools was increasing from 36.9 per cent in 1950 to 92.9 per cent in 1980 (NIER, 1988, p. 81), the suicide rate was decreasing from 32 per 100,000 15–19-year-olds in 1955 to 9 in 1970. Furthermore, school-related motives for suicide among those under the age of 21 accounted, in the first six months of 1977, for only one-quarter of juvenile suicides. Of these 106 suicides, 15 involved children aged 12–14 and 91 were committed by those aged 15–19. In other words, juvenile suicide does not seem to be linked in any consistent way with young people's first experience of *juken jigoku* in Japan, whatever the popular mythology might maintain. In fact, although Japan leads the world in educational achievement in mathematics and science, it is far from being a world leader in school violence and juvenile suicide.

Lower secondary education in Japan is formal, factual and frequently teacher-centred. The pressures on 14-year-olds caused by taking entrance examinations to upper secondary schools are the subject of much criticism but it is difficult to imagine radical change occurring in a system that is so firmly entrenched in Japanese school culture. The system, which is centrally organized, generates high levels of motivation but encourages rote learning and endless testing. Interestingly, education in England and Wales, since the passing of the Education Reform Act 1988 (referred to earlier) is becoming more centrally controlled than for many decades. A national curriculum is being implemented, programmes of study organized, attainment targets set and tests developed (DES, 1989b). In these respects it might appear at first sight that British education is moving towards the Japanese model but crucial differences remain between the two systems. As we have already noted, nearly 70 per cent of Britain's young people leave school at 16 (although 17 per cent attend Colleges of Further Education), whereas more than 90 per cent of Japan's students stay at school until they are 18. Again, a recent report in Britain by Her Majesty's Inspectorate (DES, 1989a) questions whether the Education Reform Act can be implemented successfully given the shortage of teachers in mathematics, science, design and technology and foreign languages and the generally low morale of the profession. In Japan, by contrast, teachers are respected and well rewarded and there are no shortages in crucial subject areas. The word *sensei* (teacher) is a term of respect, first- and final-year teacher salaries are generally higher than for other professions, and there is strong competition for every classroom opening. Interestingly, although teachers in Japan have been respected for centuries, it is only recently that they have gained a high economic status (Leestma *et al.*,1987, p. 19). It would appear that the Japanese government accepts that teachers play a crucial role in producing what is arguably the most literate and numerate workforce in the world and is willing to pay the price to secure a well-qualified and well-motivated profession.

However, it is not only the Japanese government that is prepared to pay the price for education. Lower secondary school students work immensely hard and have a saying: 'sleep four hours and you'll pass; sleep five hours and you'll fail' (Cox, 1983). Parents, too, may have sleepless nights because if their children fail to enter one of the prefectural high schools then they will be committed to paying fees to a local private school. Ironically, Rohlen's (1983, p. 128) studies suggest that 'because there is a solid correlation between poverty and poor school performance, it follows that the costs of private schooling are likely to fall heavily on families least able to afford them'. This association between the relatively poor and private education is not normally made in Britain or the United States because in the West private education is usually perceived as a perquisite of wealth and privilege; with some exceptions, this is not the case in Japan. Therefore the lengths to which nearly all Japanese parents will go and the sacrifices they will make to ensure that their children receive an upper secondary school education and obtain a high school diploma are truly remarkable by any standards.

Upper secondary or high school education (grades 10–12)

Until the age of 15, Japanese children experience an education of remarkable uniformity. This is ensured by a national curriculum, approved textbooks, strict adherence to schemes of work, the rotation of teachers among schools, evenness of funding, the standardization of buildings and a determination of central government, dating from the Meiji restoration, to deliver a unified and universal education for all. There are, in addition, other characteristics of Japanese society which contribute strongly to uniformity of educational opportunity. Compared with many plural societies in the West, for example, 'Japan has a population that is racially, ethnically and linguistically homogeneous' (Rohlen, 1983, p. 112).

Japan, it is true, has a small ethnic minority of Korean immigrants, who account for less than 1 per cent of the population, and a rather larger underclass, the Burakumin, who account for more than 2 per cent. The Koreans are well assimilated into society but few are Japanese citizens. They originally entered the country in the early part of the twentieth century when the Japanese ruled their homeland, but then stayed on. The Burakumin, by contrast, are Japanese but were regarded in the Tokugawa era as untouchables by reason of their lowly trades. They were given nominal emancipation in the Meiji era but were never integrated into mainstream society. Shimahara (1984) graphically chronicles their recent history and their struggle for true emancipation, resulting in the Special Measures Law for Assimilation Projects of 1969. He also demonstrates how the last 20 years have seen the Burakumin make significant economic and educational advances that might yet result in social and educational equality. Thus although minority groups exist in Japan and tensions are experienced, they are not on the same scale as in many other countries and there is some prospect of improvement.

A further characteristic of Japanese society that contributes to equality of opportunity is the more even distribution of incomes than is common in the West. This is particularly apparent in the case of the poorest fifth of the population, which has a greater share of the nation's income than its counterparts in many Western democracies. At the same time levels of unemployment are low, especially among the young, and housing is more uniform than in the West, with a marked absence of contrast between affluent and poor centres of population. Finally, marriage as an institution is more stable in Japan than in the West, in so far as stability can be measured by divorce rates, with the corollary that the incidence of single-parent families and illegitimate births is also lower.

There is, therefore, an egalitarian quality about the nine years' compulsory education in Japan which is supported by many features of national life. It is possible for parents to opt out of state-maintained schools but less than 1 per cent at the elementary level and 3 per cent at the lower secondary level actually exercise that choice, although a considerable number invest in *juku*, especially as their children grow older. However, with graduation from compulsory lower secondary and entry into voluntary upper secondary education a crucial move is made by nearly all 14-year-olds which shapes their lives for evermore. Indeed, this particular transition is more portentous of educational and career life chances than any other in Japan, for entry to the best high schools guarantees entry to the best universities which in turn guarantees entry to the best careers. Doubtless this principle holds true in many countries but in most the general run of secondary schools is seen as a rather homogeneous whole. In Japan, however, *all* the high schools in any given district are carefully and accurately ranked by the local population in terms of their ability to gain entry into higher education for their students. Thus egalitarianism in education fades and competition takes over as the race for entry into higher education begins in earnest in the nation's upper secondary schools.

Twenty years before Rohlen, in the mid-1970s, conducted his definitive fieldwork in high schools in Kobe, the ranking of schools was clear. The best schools in the area were the public high schools, and no academically able scholar would be attracted to a private school. But the meteoric rise of Nada was to change all that and to presage further changes in the status of public high schools throughout the country. On the face of it, Nada was an unlikely choice for a top private school for it was founded in the 1920s out of the profits of three *sake* brewers. At first it was more famous for its judo teams than its scholars but its star began to rise in the 1950s when the redrawing of catchment areas for some of Kobe's best public schools led to the exclusion of some able students who turned instead to Nada. Success bred success and within a decade it had become a top high school, which in Japan is measured strictly according to the criterion of the number of students placed in Tokyo University. Since the chances of a student at Nada entering Tokyo University are nearly evens, compared with an average high school student's chances of over four hundred to one, it is easy to understand this particular private school's pre-eminence.

Rohlen (1983) found Nada an unprepossessing school and one that was not lavishly equipped. In addition, classes were large and teachers old but students were bright and self-confident. Most had entered Nada directly from elementary school, where they were numbered among the top 1 per cent in ability, but a few had taken a fiercely competitive examination at 14. Whatever their age at entry, students had come to Nada to pursue a highly instrumental route to a top university to be followed by a top career at national or even international level. Nada, because it is a private school, is largely unaffected by changes in official educational policy and is therefore free to provide the services so ardently desired by its students. It offers, for example, an accelerated programme in which the national curriculum is completed with a year in hand so that the final twelfth grade can be devoted to examination preparation. In Rohlen's (1983, p. 20) experience, this final summary year provided opportunities for discussion and debate between teachers and precocious Nada boys of a quality he had never before witnessed in Japan. Nada, however, is not the only elite school in Japan.

Elite schools come in various forms. In Tokyo, where some top private schools take students from 6 to 18 years of age, competition begins in earnest at kindergarten to ensure a place on this privileged route to Tokyo University. Outside Tokyo, 12-year elite schools are mainly found attached to university departments of education where they provide a laboratory situation for prospective teachers and their tutors. These schools are publicly funded but are largely independent administratively and are free, therefore, to emulate private schools in aims and teaching methods. Other top private schools, like Nada, provide six-year secondary courses with a restricted entry at the upper secondary level. However, what all these schools have in common is a growing dominance in the battle to place students at Tokyo University, but at the expense of the public high schools. This is reflected in the league tables which are drawn up for this express purpose by the media and which are avidly studied and debated by the education-conscious Japanese public. In the 1950s public high schools held most of the top ten places and had taught over 90 per cent of students entering Tokyo University but by the 1980s the private schools occupied most of the top 15 places and had taught about half of Tokyo's freshers. A case in point is Hibiya public senior high school in Tokyo. In the 1950s and the 1960s Hibiya was a top public high school in terms of placing its graduates in Tokyo University because it could draw on the most able students from a large area of the city. But in the 1970s the realignment of catchment areas and the rise of the elite private schools robbed it of its pre-eminent position and as a consequence its name no longer adorns the top 20 in the annual rankings.

At the upper secondary level about 24 per cent of all schools are private and these enrol about 28 per cent of all high school students.

Private schools are concentrated in the cities and are consequently thin on the ground in rural areas. They differ considerably in quality. Leestma *et al.* (1987, p. 41) identify between 50 and 100 top private secondary schools out of a total of 1,300 and suggest that in any given area the 'best' high school may be either public or private. The remaining public high schools will be strictly ranked according to the success of their graduates in entering higher education, as will, in their turn, the private schools. Where a previously 'best' public high school has had its catchment area reduced to its immediate local neighbourhood in order to bring about a more equitable distribution of very bright children in a given city, some parents will have reacted by moving their children into private schools; but, generally speaking, the public high schools are preferred by parents because they are perceived as offering a good-quality academic education at an affordable price.

Upper secondary education in Japan is neither compulsory, although over 90 per cent of Japanese children attend high school, nor is it free. The fees at public high school work out at about £300 per year but those at private school are substantially higher. They are not, however, as high as English 'public' schools because the Japanese government subsidizes private education. The costs of running schools in Britain and Japan are broadly comparable; therefore, according to Lynn's (1988, p. 40) rule of thumb, if in 1990 it costs £3000 per annum to send a British child to a private day secondary school, then in Japan, where parents pay approximately 60 per cent of school fees, it will cost about £1800. However, it is not helpful to compare British and Japanese private schools apart from their costs.

The private sector in Japan, which educates 28 per cent of upper secondary school students, is much *larger* than its British and American counterparts, which account for 6 and 13 per cent, respectively. Furthermore, private education for most students in Japan covers a much *shorter* period of time than in the West because most of the above 28 per cent do not begin private education until the official school leaving age of fifteen. In Japan, therefore, of those who opt for private education, the vast majority spend only three years in the private sector, compared with seven or eleven years in Britain. Again private education in Japan is more indicative of student academic merit than parental income, although the latter is clearly implicated. Nada, for example, is the most famous school in Japan and yet its fees are about average for a private school. It is run on a shoestring budget, offers no scholarships and receives little in the way of contributions from its alumni. Entry to Nada depends entirely on student merit, as demonstrated in entrance examinations, and family background is not taken into consideration. There is therefore, no comparison between Japan's top academic high schools and Britain's top public schools.

The latter are socially exclusive, with family background and wealth counting for a good deal. They offer some scholarships on a merit basis but the majority of students pay substantial fees. In Britain, therefore, merit alone rarely gains a student entry to a top public school, whereas in Japan merit is both a necessary and usually sufficient reason for the best private education. In both countries, however, lack of merit in children can also be a cause for parents seeking private education; but whereas in Britain the cost for this remedial task is usually borne by the better off, in Japan it tends to fall on those who can least afford it.

Rohlen (1983) studied in some detail five high schools in the Kobe area, from Nada, the top private school, at one extreme to Sakura, a lowly vocational night school, at the other. In the middle ranks he surveyed two public high schools and a vocational high school. He was able to assess the family background of second-year or eleventh-grade students in these schools according to their number of siblings, working mothers, missing parents, own room for study, *juku* attendance, father with university education and parents who were Korean or Burakumin. The results of this survey are instructive.

Japan, perhaps more nearly than any other nation, approaches the ideal of equal educational opportunity for all, with students' futures decided by their academic merit. Unsurprisingly, however, evidence for a purely meritocratic social system was not forthcoming from Rohlen's survey. Instead, the inequalities which inhibit progress in realizing the ideal around the world showed up with characteristic regularity. Thus students at Nada have a study at home in which to work, have on average one sibling and enjoy the presence of both parents. They have mothers who are unlikely to work outside the home and fathers who are likely to have attended university. A student at Nada is very likely to attend *juku* and will be neither Korean nor Burakumin, but he will be male. A student at Sakura technical night high school, on the other hand, has only an even chance of working in his own study space and may have on average two siblings to distract him. His father is unlikely to have attended university and there is a one in seven chance that one parent will be missing. There is a one is three chance that his mother will be working and that he will attend *juku*, and a one in twenty chance that he will be Burakumin. In fact, the sharpest differentiation in the survey was between the three academic and the two vocational schools. Academic children were far more likely to have academic fathers than vocational children and vocational children were more likely than academic children to have parents who belonged to minority groups and who followed lowly occupations.

Japanese education presents, then, something of a paradox because that longer part which is compulsory and which encourages unity and social harmony is followed by this shorter part which is voluntary and yet which divides the young of any given locality into the most finely graded and delicately pared of all social hierarchies. Furthermore, this division has about it an air of finality because it has been intimated to students many times over through countless test results in the junior high school years and it will be reinforced time and time again in the social and occupational realities of post-high school life. In addition, the educational system is widely perceived as being objective and fair with differences in outcome attributed to the differential efforts of the students. Thus even where social class differences are admitted the effects of these are held to be more the responsibility of the parents concerned than of the schools. In other words, the schools are seen to be even-handed and to be operating policies which neither favour the rich nor target the poor. And yet the growth in private education, epitomized by the rise of Nada, clearly *does* favour the better off, however reluctant the Japanese are to make this connection in the naked terms commonly employed in the West. It would seem, however, that the long formative years in compulsory education, during which schools strive and are seen to strive for equality of educational opportunity, legitimize the multi-layered divisions which occur at high school level. Evidence for this statement can be found in Rohlen's description of life at the Sakura technical night high school.

Students at Sakura gather for lessons at an hour when the vast majority of high school pupils are either at home or travelling homewards. Most will have been at some manual work during the day but some will have come from shops or offices. None will be in school uniforms. Absenteeism at Sakura is high, with only about half of those enrolled attending regularly. Many students struggle so hard to read their own language in literature classes or to master electronics in vocational periods that their attention span is short and their behaviour discourteous by the normal, exacting Japanese standards. Nevertheless, by dint of hard work and regular attendance some students will attain a sufficient level of literacy to enter a junior college or a low-ranking private university. This achievement speaks volumes for the popularity of education in Japan and the very high motivation of its students. In 1985, for example, 92 per cent of 15–17-year-olds were enrolled in upper secondary or high school education (NIER, 1988, p. 2), whereas in England and Wales the latest official statistics (DES 1988b) show that only 32 per cent of 16–18-year-olds were in full-time education. In fact only 17 per cent attended school but nearly as many again were in further or higher education. A further 15 per cent took part in Youth Training Schemes, 43 per cent were employed and 9 per cent unemployed. Indeed, to quote a City and Guilds of London Institute (1987) document, 'the United Kingdom is the only major industrial economy where the majority of young people expect to start work at sixteen'. In Japan less than 3 per cent seek employment at 15 and the majority (around 70 per cent in 1984) follow an academic programme leading to college entrance examinations: youth unemployment at this age is negligible.

Academic high schools, both public and private, represent the main route through upper secondary education in Japan. The public high schools are in the majority and provide about 70 per cent of the students at institutions of higher education. Japanese upper secondary school buildings, like those of their junior high school counterparts, are simple and unadorned. Their primary purpose is to house cohorts of serious young people intent on obtaining a good secondary education and, if. at all possible, admission to university. To this end, the buildings contain all that is necessary in terms of libraries, laboratories, gymnasia, sports facilities and audio-visual aids but little else. Interestingly Rohlen (1983, p. 36) found that Okada public high school, which enjoyed a very good academic reputation in Kobe, was housed in decrepit old buildings in much need of repair. But, whatever the age of school buildings or students, it is the latter that clean the former after every school day.

At the upper secondary school level, over 80 per cent of the teachers are male with female teachers restricted generally to subjects such as home economics and girls' physical education. Lessons, like those at lower secondary school, frequently resemble 50-minute lectures. Rohlen (1983, p. 13) admits that his self-imposed task of participant observer was often extremely tedious. The teachers were well prepared but were also extremely serious. They seldom departed from the prescribed text for the day and practically never introduced visual aids or instigated discussion. They did, however, make reference to impending tests. Most students took careful notes during lessons but some engaged in universal and time-honoured pupil behaviours such as gazing out of the window, passing notes and looking at carefully concealed magazines. However, there was no overt indiscipline during lessons and the expression of high spirits was reserved for ten-minute breaks between classes and after-school activities.

This careful rationing of youthful exuberance is a feature of Japanese education throughout all 12 grades, with the rules clearly understood by both teachers and taught. Thus good-natured high spirits between and after classes is clearly perceived by both parties as a corollary of quiet conformity during lessons. Possibly as a result of this agreed and accepted dichotomy, real indiscipline is rare in schools. Nevertheless, Japanese school children can and do have great fun at school and they are certainly not the dour automatons described by those who have seen them only at lessons. There is, however, no disguising the seriousness of the teachers.

As a rule instruction at upper secondary school is highly instrumental and is designed to facilitate university entrance. To this end, lessons are formal and factual and are designed to introduce students to large areas of new material. The good teacher, therefore, is perceived as the one who conscientiously covers the ground as laid down in the course of study. He, or less frequently she, will not attach as much value as colleagues in the West to enriching this basic diet with supplementary material, audio-visual aids and challenging questions, although it is possible that younger teachers are developing more flexible approaches.

The curriculum of the upper secondary school is as demanding as anything that has gone before. It is geared to university entrance and although fewer than one in five high school students will actually attend university, the desire to obtain some form of higher education is present in nearly all boys and not a few girls. University education in Japan confers a lifetime's advantage on those who obtain it. The more prestigious the university attended the more likely one is to gain a first appointment with a prestigious organization. Subsequent advancement, too, is dependent quite as much on one's original university as on any other factor. Therefore the competition to enter the best universities is most severe and students who have spent their lower secondary school years striving to enter the best possible high school now spend their upper secondary school years straining to enter the best possible university for universities, like high schools, are carefully graded and ranked. Tokyo University stands supreme and offers the best possible start to a distinguished career. It heads the first division of about a dozen institutions which include the remaining five former imperial universities, a handful of public universities, a technological university and two private institutions. The second division is larger than the first, comprising about forty institutions, but like the first it is dominated by the public universities. The public universities are better funded than their private counterparts and, like the public high schools, offer good facilities in return for modest fees. The private universities, on the other hand, apart from some notable exceptions, are not so highly regarded since they are obliged to charge substantial fees for an inferior product. Yet the public universities can take only 20 per cent of the student population so that the remaining eighty per cent of students need to pay substantial fees to obtain any form of higher education.

This book is specifically about Japanese *schools* but it is necessary to appreciate the dream of nearly all Japanese parents that their children attend university in order to understand the participation rates of over 90 per cent in upper secondary education and the dominance in academic high schools of a curriculum designed for university entrants. In fact, the first year of high school for both academic and vocational students is virtually identical. The study of the Japanese language continues, in both its modern and classical forms, along with mathematics and science. Since English was the almost universal elective in lower secondary school it is continued at high school but with six rather than three periods per week. 'Contemporary society' replaces moral education but its study of contemporary world-wide issues includes personal ethics. Health and physical education lessons take up five periods a week for boys because they drop industrial arts at high school, but girls continue with home economics and enjoy therefore only three health and physical education periods per week. Music and calligraphy, homeroom and club activities continue as before, but the first mentioned now only rates one period per week.

The second year of high school marks a break between academic and vocational studies and between academic students who opt for literature and those who opt for science. In the 28 per cent of high schools that are organized as comprehensive schools, these two breaks occur under the same roof, but more commonly students are separated at 15 into academic high schools (49 per cent) and vocational high schools (23 per cent) (Leestma *et al.*, 1987, p. 41). Vocational high schools will be discussed separately below. In fact the break in academic high schools between literature and science courses is not so great. While the literature students continue to take maths and science, though for a reduced number of periods, the science students continue with Japanese language and history as well as English, likewise for fewer periods than before. Even in the third and final year of high school a student's education continues to be both broadly based and demanding. Arts students study modern as well as classical literature and are introduced to ethics or politics but they still continue with maths and science for four periods a week. Science students are introduced to integral and differential calculus, probability and statistics and continue with physics and chemistry, but they also study modern literature and English for nine periods per week. However, in Japan, the hoped for result of one's striving to master the school curriculum is not success in a public examination such as the English and Welsh A levels but success in the entrance examination of the university of one's choice. There does exist a standardized entrance examination but many universities use it only for screening purposes while retaining their own examination as the instrument of final assessment. Therefore students at high school need as much counselling and guidance concerning which university to enter as they did at lower secondary school when choosing their high school.

Guidance and counselling are provided by the school and more specifically by *yobiko*, a specialized form of *juku*. *Yobiko*, together with *juku*, will be discussed separately below, but first something needs to be said about the destinations of 18-year-old school leavers in Japan. In 1984, approximately 29 per cent of high school leavers went to university and junior college and a further 12 per cent attended special colleges for vocational training. Given that another 12 per cent continued with a variety of school-based vocational courses, only about 40 per cent sought employment at 18, with about 5 per cent failing to get a job (Leestma *et al.*, 1987, p. 78). In England and Wales, by contrast, 70 per cent of 18-year-olds found employment in 1988 but 12 per cent did not. This left 15 per cent attending institutions of further and higher education and 2 per cent continuing at school (DES, 1988b, Table 4). Therefore guidance and counselling in Japanese schools is geared as much to educational as to vocational guidance, whereas in England and Wales the latter predominates. Doubtless all Japanese teachers assist high school students in some way to reach their goals in employment, college or higher education, but approximately 40 per cent, in addition to their basic 15 hours a week of regular teaching, are homeroom advisers with special responsibility for students' educational, vocational and personal affairs. Each high school also has specialist vocational guidance counsellors and disciplinary officers.

By most Western standards Japanese teenagers are incredibly well behaved. Their almost unanimous desire for the highest possible level of education leads to a characteristically middle-class postponement of adult interests and activities, which is reinforced by the high levels of control exercised by school and home. School control extends even beyond the boundaries of the building to matters such as appropriate dress and behaviour in the neighbourhood, but in this matter as in most others the schools are invariably supported by the parents. Adolescent rebellion, therefore, when it does occur, is reminiscent more of England 50 years ago than of contemporary British youth behaviour. Rebellion is often limited to small but significant adjustments to school uniform and hairstyles and manifests itself most seriously in cigarette smoking. Students caught smoking in the streets, for example, are taken by the police to the police station where parents and school disciplinary officers will also be summoned. Repeated smoking offences can give adequate grounds for expulsion from high school. Adolescent drinking in Japan is rare, drug-taking is almost unknown and car-driving is not permissible before 18. Sixteen-year-olds may drive small motor-bikes but most schools discourage their use and students, like most Japanese, use public transport. In mainstream academic high schools, then, there is comparatively little serious indiscipline, but greater problems may exist in vocational high schools.

As we have seen, approximately 70 per cent of all full-time upper secondary school students attend academic high schools, with the remaining 30 per cent receiving vocational education. In the early 1950s when less than half the relevant age group attended high schools, vocational schools were oversubscribed and their courses highly valued because graduation led to enhanced pay and employment prospects. However, with the growing popularity of academic high schools in the 1960s and 1970s vocational high schools declined in popularity and began to gain a reputation for being institutions for the less able and more difficult pupils. Certainly Rohlen (1983, p. 37) paints a vivid if not lurid picture of life at Yama Commercial High School, where morale was low because few students had positively chosen to attend the school. Indeed, according to Rohlen, the majority had failed entrance examinations to academic high school, had parents who could not afford to pay private school fees and were therefore inattentive in class because they had so little prospect of achieving the Japanese ideal of a higher education and every prospect of obtaining the least ideal, which is a low-status job for life. In consequence, breaches of school rules were more overt than at academic schools, with cigarette butts left on lavatory floors and motor-bikes ridden openly in out-of-school hours. Cantor (1989, p. 13), in a recent comparative study of vocational education and training, confirms one or two aspects of Rohlen's appraisal of vocational schools. For example, he notes that there is little competition to enter one particular vocational high school in Tokyo since there are 'usually only as many applicants as places'. This situation, of course, stands in stark contrast to the oversubscription of public academic high schools and is a fair indicator of the popularity level of vocational high schools. Cantor also notes the relatively higher drop-out rate from vocational high schools — a further indicator that motivation is more difficult to maintain in this sector. However, both Cantor (1989, p. 12) and Prais (1986, p. 133) reject the notion that vocational high schools cater only for those of low academic ability. Prais, in particular, quotes an unpublished study from the National Institute of Educational Research in Tokyo which indicates that there is a much wider spread of ability in the vocational schools — and indeed, the academic high schools, too — than the popular mythology would allow. It would appear, therefore, that Rohlen's description of Yama Commercial High School reflects faithfully the universal Cinderella-like status of vocational education, together with an ugly-sister-like omission of a number of its intrinsic virtues.

There are six major courses of study that can be followed at vocational high school. The smallest take-up is for fisheries and health, followed by home economics and agriculture, with the most popular courses being industrial (or technical) and commercial studies, the former attracting chiefly boys and the latter girls. Thus commercial high schools, like Yama High School, are the most popular of all. As we have already seen, the programme of study in the first year of high school is much the same whether students are following an academic or a vocational course. Thereafter a general academic course remains the core curriculum in vocational schools, with students spending around 16 hours a week studying Japanese, mathematics, social studies, English and science and, in addition, nine hours a week, like their counterparts in the academic high schools, on health and physical education, home economics, music or art, and homeroom or club activities. The actual time devoted to vocational education, therefore, is around ten hours a week or one-third of the timetable. This broad-based approach to vocational education is consistent with the Japanese philosophy of education which is neatly encapsulated by Chris Hayes *et al.* (1984, p. 4), who conclude that in Japan 'specialization is avoided at all educational levels' and that stress is placed on the fundamentals, particularly the three Rs.

However, that part of the upper secondary curriculum that *is* vocational is also specialized. Prais (1986, p. 136) explains this apparent contradiction in the following manner. He notes that the prevailing ideology is that Japanese schools, including vocational high schools, develop general abilities while industry trains in specific skills, yet he finds on examining syllabuses and textbooks that 'the instruction provided in . . . technical and commercial schools is . . . quite as specific, and as close to practical reality, as in comparable English, French and German courses'. He gives some examples. 'The *machinery* course covers in immense detail the many standard types of milling cutters, and the precise contours of the many standard types of gear wheels' and 'the *electricity* course details the multitudinous types of insulators available for carrying high tension cables'. Prais also points out that before graduating from vocational high schools students may take highly specialized trade tests such as 'Registered Boiler Technician, Gas Welding Technician, Senior Electric Technician . . . Bookkeeping Licence' and 'Information Processing Technician'. Additionally, Prais finds that students on the machinery course are given a broad technological overview that includes skills (e.g., technical drawing and basic fitting techniques) that would constitute separate, free-standing courses in England.

Prais (1986, p. 137) found, however, that the most telling difference between England and Japan with regard to vocational education was that, even allowing for an English workforce half the size of the Japanese, the Japanese are producing many more students at a comparable level than the English, given that the vocational high school courses are roughly equivalent to the British Business and Technician Education Council (BTEC) National Diplomas. Thus, in mechanical courses, electrical and electronic courses and in business studies courses, the Japanese produce 10–20 times more people at technician level per head of the workforce than the English. It is true, of course, that in Japan there is no national council equivalent to the

BTEC and that the vocational high school diploma is awarded to those students whose achievements are judged satisfactory solely by the school they attend; but as in Japan all upper secondary school students attend voluntarily, and consequently all parents pay fees of some sort, both school officials and consumers have a distinct interest in the quality of the product. Naturally there will be variations in quality of instruction between schools and in ability between students but it is difficult to escape the evidence of international tests of academic achievement which suggest that the Japanese are particularly successful in educating and training students of average ability and of bringing the least academically able up to minimum standards of literacy and numeracy.

However, this particular success story in vocational education possesses little glamour and is not much reported in the literature. For example, Hayes *et al.* (1984, p. 45) stress the quality of general education rather than the value of vocational education in Japan because major employers 'recruit people into membership of the organization rather than occupations'. McCormick (1988, p. 42) agrees and believes that the same major employers recruit blue-collar workers more on the basis of their ability and potential to update skills in the light of technological change than on any particular skills that they may have learnt at school. However, Prais (1986, p. 132) addresses the question of what happens in the mass of small firms, which often make components for the larger firms, where funds for training programmes are limited. His answer is that they employ the graduates of vocational high schools who come to them with twelve years' general education, including two years' technical training, which places them at a level somewhere between machine operatives and engineers. Prais (1986, p. 123) further identifies a lack of people with this level of education and skill in Britain. He cites discussions with Japanese-owned businesses in Britain and quotes the experience of one firm in particular whose Japanese-made advanced automatic machines were operating at only 60 per cent of their level of capability. The problem lay not in the availability of skilled engineers nor in the supply of unskilled British labour, but in the dearth of people at an intermediate level 'who were technically trained and willing to carry out routine operating procedures, able to notice in advance when anything might cause trouble and capable of routine maintenance of their complex machines'. In a nutshell, this dearth is a real British problem and one cause of our industrial weakness compared with the Japanese, who are able to prepare vocationally to the age of 18 and beyond those in the middle and lower reaches of the ability range.

Yet vocational education in upper secondary schools in Japan is in decline, with the number of pupils falling at the rate of about 1 per cent per year since the beginning of the 1970s, while at the same time the percentage of those attending academic high schools is rising, spurred on no doubt by the dream of going to university. A second avenue to vocational education through *technical colleges* is at best static. Sixty-two of these colleges, based on the British model, were founded in the 1960s but there are no plans to increase this number. They were designed to meet the needs of a rapidly expanding industrial economy by offering five-year courses, largely in engineering, to 15-year-old lower secondary school graduates. They presently attract less than 1 per cent, almost all male, of the target age group. Hayes *et al.* (1984, p. 4) dismiss them rather peremptorily as 'the system's biggest failures' but Cantor (1989, p. 16) reports favourably on the Tokyo National College of Technology. He found severe competition for places, a very low drop-out rate and good employment prospects for its graduates. However, the College of Technology in Tokyo is one of the most highly regarded and may indeed be able to produce technologists rather than technicians, with all the associated career differentials that these terms imply, but its counterparts across the country may be less successful in emulating Tokyo and therein may lie their failure to attract potential technologists. A third and final avenue to vocational education, the *special training schools* and *miscellaneous schools*, is booming. The former are largely for graduates from upper secondary schools and are therefore outside the scope of this present volume, while largest single group in the latter is the *yobiko*, which offer intense training to high school students for university entrance examinations, and will therefore be discussed below. Most schools in both categories are privately run and perhaps what they demonstrate more than anything else is the remarkable enthusiasm of the Japanese for education and their willingness to pay for it. However, vocational education and training in schools represents only the tip of the iceberg in Japan, where industry, in its zeal to remain up to date and competitive, is responsible for the lion's share. For the interested reader, Cantor's (1989) timely volume is recommended as a lucid guide to this vital topic.

Upper secondary education in Japan is, then, remarkably popular, with 92 per cent of the relevant age group enrolled in academic or vocational high schools in 1985 (NIER, 1988, p. 2). In Britain, by contrast, only 32 per cent of all 16–18-year-olds were engaged in full-time education at school or in further or higher education in 1988, although a further 15 per cent participated in Youth Training Schemes (DES, 1988b, Table 1). The simple fact is that in Britain the majority of young people leave school as soon as they can, whereas in Japan the majority stay on voluntarily for a further three years during which they follow a broad and nationally agreed curriculum. This means that *all* high school students continue to study their own language, English, mathematics, science, humanities, social studies and the arts until they are 18. So although both the Japanese and the British succeed handsomely in educating their brightest young people, few would deny that the Japanese succeed far better that the British in educating the average pupil and those who are below average in ability but who nevertheless go on to become vital members of the workforce. The economic consequences that flow from this crucial difference between the two countries must be very considerable, yet one reason for the difference is easily found. The Japanese have both an enormous enthusiasm for education and also a willingness to pay for the advantages it confers. Thus all parents pay some fees for their children's upper secondary education, and some parents whose children fail to enter public high schools pay a good deal for private education. However, the state subsidizes private education at this level both in terms of capital grants to schools and also by paying around 50 per cent of the teachers' salary bill. It is this degree of enthusiasm for and commitment to education by both parents and government that accounts for participation rates in schools up to the age of 18 that are running at three times British levels. It follows that Japanese levels of literacy and numeracy exceed British levels, too.

The Japanese system of education is by no means purely meritocratic although it may approach that ideal more closely than in most industrialized countries. Thus the high school entrance examination by which those entering upper secondary education are ranked hierarchically is widely perceived as objective and fair with individuals and families who experience failure being much more ready to blame their own shortcomings than those of the system. Nevertheless, the formal education system in Japan which is so highly regarded by its consumers is supplemented in a quite unique way by a privately run informal system which provides tuition for those who can pay at all stages of their educational career but most particularly at two stages — high school entrance and university entrance.

Juku and yobiko

Non-formal education is always likely to exist alongside a formal education system where children want or need extra instruction outside school hours or where parents think that their children need extra tuition, but it is doubtful whether any other nation has developed private supplementary education on the scale that is found in Japan. The *juku* phenomenon is a market response to a perceived educational need and it attracts no government grant or subsidy at all. It is a further measure of Japanese enthusiasm for education, or Japanese anxiety about educational achievement, and it is certainly a sign that the Japanese are willing to pay for educational assistance and advantage. Lynn (1988, p. 24) seems to see *juku* only in terms of their ability to confer educational advantages on the children of the middle classes, but this is a rather simplistic summary of the diversity of provision that is available and the variety of needs that lead children to attend *juku*. Yuuki (1987, p. 23), for example, gives three main reasons for the popularity of *juku*. The first is indeed a frank statement that *juku* are used to enhance academic performance in a country where one's social status depends to a considerable extent on one's academic background in terms of level of education attained and institutions attended. However, the second reason underlines the fact that a strong spirit of egalitarianism in compulsory school education means that in practice much of the teaching is addressed to the 'average' child with correspondingly little attention paid to individuals who may be bored because they are familiar with the material or to children who are struggling because a combination of below average ability, automatic promotion and a system that does not allow for remedial education has left them far behind. This second group, the *ochikobore*, are seeking not so much enhancement as help in keeping up with an extremely demanding curriculum. The third of Yuuki's reasons for *juku* relates to the increasing number of urban nuclear families where both parents are at work and where *juku* can provide children with assistance in their school study programmes that their parents are unable to give. Doubtless there are also many homes where only one parent is at work but the assistance of *juku* is still valued as children grapple with school programmes that the parents also find difficult to understand. In addition to these academic reasons for attending *juku*, it is likely that there are also social reasons. Indeed, evidence exists that many children like the opportunity to make friends outside their school circle and, in the case of smaller *juku*, have more personal contact with teachers (Leestma *et al.*, 1987, p. 11). The size of *juku* is enormously varied and ranges from small domestic groups of two or three pupils to large commercial enterprises catering for over a thousand students.

The greatest number of *juku* are supplementary or *hoshu-juku*. They are mostly founded by individuals, tend to be small in size and concentrate their efforts on shadowing the school curriculum both in repeating past lessons and in preparing students for future ones. The largest *juku* are preparatory or *shingaku-juku*. They tend to be owned by big business organizations and concentrate specifically on preparing students for entrance examinations to prestigious junior or senior high schools. Since the *shingaku-juku* specialize in high achievers they often have entrance examinations of their own to discover whether candidates can profit from their services, for *shingaku-juku* do not simply shadow the regular school curriculum but enlarge upon it and enrich it. This rich academic diet may have the desired effect of enhancing entrance examination performance, but it may also lead in bright pupils to disenchantment with regular school lessons. Comprehensive or *sogo-juku*, as the name implies, combine the aims of both the above-mentioned types of *juku*, although they generally exhibit a bias towards preparatory courses. However, not all students can stand the pace in Japanese schools and for them there are relief or *kyusai-juku*. These provide the individualized approach to learning that the regular schools do not and offer relief to the emotionally handicapped, the delinquent and those with school phobia. *Kyusai-juku* are often small and, unlike their prosperous cousins, often experience financial problems. Academic *juku* are largely a post-war phenomenon but *juku* specializing in abacus calculation, calligraphy, musical and sports skills belong to a much older tradition and are particularly popular among elementary school children. However, at the elementary level of academic *juku*, arithmetic, Japanese and English are the most popular subjects, but at the lower secondary level English is the most popular (a compulsory 'elective' for most students) followed by mathematics. At the upper secondary level there are fewer *juku* classes because the academic high school population is approximately 70 per cent of the total high school population and *yobiko*, a form of *juku* specializing in university entrance, offers supplementary education to high school students.

Juku instructors are often young, part-time college students or graduates without formal educational qualifications, but a number of the full-time instructors are former teachers who are critical of regular school. State school teachers, however, are no longer permitted to moonlight at *juku*. Instructors from the principal down are usually well qualified, well paid and keen to offer more individualized teaching in small groups than is available in school. *Juku* are available six or seven days a week and preparatory or *shingaku-juku* open during the school summer holiday. Classes begin when regular school closes in the afternoon and finish at nine, ten or even eleven o'clock at night. I was astonished to see school children in uniform in Tokyo travelling home by train at these late hours still clutching their briefcases and reading their textbooks. The cost of *juku* varies according to the level of instruction given from grade one to nine and the type of *juku* attended, with preparatory supplementary instruction being the most expensive. Ejima (1988, p. 55) suggests an average cost for *juku* for a child at elementary school of about £800 a year, and for a child at lower secondary school about £1000. However, when considering these costs one has to bear in mind that the average income of a Japanese family amounts to about £33,000 per annum. Nevertheless, it is likely that over 40 per cent of the school population nation-wide do not use academic *juku* at all, not even during the last year of junior high school when they are preparing for high school entrance examinations. For some the reason might be cost but more common reasons probably include beliefs about children enjoying their childhood and having sufficient time for play and relaxation.

Juku are widely criticized both for reinforcing the worst aspects of the Japanese educational system and for undermining its considerable strengths (Yuuki, 1987, p. 29). Thus it is seen as further intensifying an already intensive entrance examination contest to prestigious junior and senior high schools and as legitimizing the importance that is attached to elite educational institutions in determining an individual's career and life chances. It is seen again as interfering with both the teaching and club activities of regular school as well as affecting adversely the life and culture of children. Certainly one of the arguments against reducing the Japanese school week to five days is that it would make more time available for children to study at home and attend *juku*. Finally critics say that *juku* undermine the egalitarian and meritocratic qualities of Japanese education by offering extra tuition and guidance to those who can best afford it. However, *juku* do not stand alone. They are to high school entrance what *yobiko* is to university entrance; and since the ranking of high schools is linked ineluctably to the hierarchical structure of universities, *juku* and *yobiko* are widely perceived as the two major non-formal avenues to educational progress in Japan.

Yobiko is a specialized form of *shingaku-juku* which exists to prepare students for the last major hurdle in their academic lives — university entrance. Curiously, although some senior high school students do attend *yobiko* for help in achieving this aim, it is high school graduates (*ronin*) for whom *yobiko* is chiefly intended. *Ronin* are literally *samurai* without a lord and the term, therefore, dates from the Tokugawa era. It is particularly exemplified by one famous event frequently portrayed on the Kabuki stage and on television, where at the turn of the eighteenth century, 46 *ronin* avenged the death of their murdered lord only to be commanded by the *shogun* to commit *hara-kiri* so that they could join their beloved master to whom they had shown such loyalty. The *ronin* dutifully obeyed the *shogun* and their tombs in the temple of Sengakuji in Tokyo are visited by thousands of admiring visitors every year. Contemporary *ronin* number over 200,000 each year and are similarly without a master. They have graduated from high school but have failed to gain entrance to the university of their choice, so they attend *yobiko* full-time for one year in order to improve their chances second time around. According to Tsukada (1988, p. 286), 'in 1985, the 214,127 *ronin* student applicants for universities and four-year colleges in Japan constituted 48.2% of the total applicants' and 'the percentage of entrants to the most prestigious universities . . . is considerably higher: 57.3% for the seven former imperial universities and 65% for the major private universities in 1984'. This situation has led some wags to suggest that the Japanese educational system is not so much 6-3-3-4 but 6-3-3-1-4 or even 6-3-3-*x*-4 since some *ronin* try more than once to enter the top universities via *yobiko*. The cost of *yobiko* equals that of an average year at university, about £6000 at 1990 prices, so it is likely to discriminate in favour of those whose parents enjoy a high income and vice versa. Indeed Tsukada (1988, p. 300) found that *yobiko* basically reproduces the stratification of youthful society first revealed by the high school entrance examination and that 'those who can choose *yobiko* preparation as a second chance frequently come from prestigious high schools, which often require families of means to support examination preparation and school placement from the pre-high school years onward'. It is true that because of the sheer size of the Japanese higher education system, the fourth largest in the world, equality of opportunity exists to some degree; nevertheless, at the top universities like Tokyo, four out of every five students have parents with professional or executive backgrounds. Thus, although those with exceptional academic merit may find their way unassisted to a top Japanese university, the path is made considerably easier for a child, particularly a male child, who comes from a wealthy home where the payment of *juku* and *yobiko* fees is not seen as a problem.

University and college education

Only the United States, the Soviet Union and India have larger post-secondary education systems than Japan, which possesses over 400 universities, over 500 junior colleges, 62 technical colleges and, in addition, numerous special training and miscellaneous schools. In fact 'more than fifty per cent of senior high school graduates continue to study at higher educational institutions of some kind or other' (Nishimura, 1985, p. 20). Generally speaking, the universities operated by the national government are the most prestigious institutions but, as we have seen, the competition to enter them is so severe that a private sector response of remarkable proportions has sprung up. Thus in the mid-1980s about 18 per cent of high school graduates went to university, about 11 per cent to junior college and about 25 per cent to establishments for vocational training (Leestma *et al.*, 1987, p. 78), but around 70 per cent of the undergraduates, 90 per cent of the college students and those attending special training colleges were at private institutions. At first, in the 1950s and 1960s, the private sector was allowed to operate without government support or direction but this led to abuses in some cases in the form of exorbitant fees and unreasonable student–teacher ratios. Government intervention and partial funding have removed some of these excesses but many private universities still operate at a disadvantage in terms of poor library facilities, high student–teacher ratios and a minimum of set written assignments. But then a remarkable feature of higher education in general in Japan is that students, having negotiated one of the most demanding school programmes in the world and having laboured to pass entrance examinations into high school and universities, begin one of the most relaxed periods of their lives, during which in the first two years at least lectures in many faculties can be cut with impunity and an unprecedented amount of time can be devoted to clubs and leisure activities. Indeed, entry to university is everything and subsequent performance matters relatively little, according to Duke (1986, p. 217), an American academic who has taught in Japanese universities. He goes no further than many other critics in claiming that only a limited number of students in a minority of Japanese universities are faced with real intellectual challenges and that the majority regard higher education as a moratorium with graduation as their right in return for their heroic efforts at school in the past and their life-long devotion to a company in the future. Japanese educators are aware of these shortcomings and are ready to discuss reforming measures, especially in the light of demographic changes that will lead to a rapid decline in student numbers in the 1990s, but so long as 'the university entrance examination is the primary sorting device for careers in Japan' (OECD, 1971, p. 89), the act of entering university will be the glittering prize rather than a student's performance once admitted.

To conclude a chapter on the restoration and development of education in Japan in the second half of the twentieth century is to invite comparison with an earlier restoration in the nineteenth century. Then the young Emperor Meiji commanded that knowledge be sought throughout the world and that emissaries be dispatched to Europe and the United States to garner information of every sort. In the twentieth century, by contrast, the middle-aged Emperor Hirohito counselled his people to endure the unendurable and to accept American solutions to his country's problems; but this second emperor lived on to see the Americans make their pilgrimage back to Japan to discover how their own educational ideas had been so transformed and transmuted that Japanese children consistently outperformed theirs in international tests of achievement. This American quest for knowledge became formalized in an agreement between Prime Minister Nakasone and President Reagan in 1984, when two studies were commissioned. The American study (Leestma *et al.*, 1987) joins a growing literature that seeks to understand the reasons for Japanese educational achievement, but the Japanese study, while praising American education for being 'rich and flexible', has not led to any real desire in Japan to learn from the American experience (Gordon, 1987, p. 4). Rather, the Japanese continue to be critical of their own educational system for being rigid, excessively uniform and dominated by entrance examinations. Prime Minister Nakasone responded to these and other criticisms by setting up an *ad hoc* National Council on Educational Reform which delivered its fourth and final report in August 1987. This report will be discussed in Chapter 5.

The Japanese success story is easily told for education is immensely popular, as can be seen by the very high participation rates, both before and after compulsory education, which far exceed those for England and Wales. Academic achievement, as measured by international tests, is also considerably higher than that found in the United States and the United Kingdom and seems to go hand in hand with highly motivated students, well-respected and well-paid teachers and a generally high expectation in society of what children are capable of doing. It would seem that, in Japan, a country poor in natural resources, the greatest possible investment has been made in its most precious human resource, its children, while in the United Kingdom, which has been richly endowed with natural resources, the education of *all* its children to the highest possible level has never been a top priority.

4

Japanese childhood and adolescence

In 1987 when I was teaching a fourth-year group of 15-year-olds at a Leicestershire comprehensive school I informed them that I was about to go to Japan to visit schools and universities and to discuss contrasting attitudes to education in England and Japan (Simmons and Wade, 1988). I began the lesson by asking the class what they or their parents possessed that was made in Japan and, with little difficulty we assembled an impressive list of products on the blackboard. I then explained to the class that their opposite numbers in Japan were at the end of their compulsory period of education and I invited guesses as to what proportion of Japanese young people would stay on at school voluntarily for a further three years. The guesses started at about the right level for English schools (15 per cent) but when I mentioned that there were other possibilities in England such as Colleges of Further Education and Youth Training Schemes the guesses rose to 50 per cent. One girl, detecting this figure was still not sufficient to bring the guessing game to an end, said resignedly: 'I suppose you're going to say that a hundred per cent of them stay on at school.' 'Very nearly', I replied, at which she exclaimed: 'Gordon Bennett!' Gordon Bennett was a term extremely popular among young people in 1987 as an expression of astonishment and surprise and it captured beautifully the genuine amazement of a group of English 15-year-olds that a country existed where the vast majority of young people voluntarily stayed on at school until they were eighteen. However, as the lesson unfolded it occurred to a few students that there might be a connection between the list of high-quality products that we had so easily written up on the board at the beginning of the period and the enthusiasm for education among Japanese young people that we were discussing.

A little over two years after this lesson, on 18 April 1989, Lord Young, the then Secretary of State for Trade and Industry, welcomed Toyota, the world's third largest car manufacturer, to Britain to build a

£700 million car factory at Burnaston, a village five miles from Derby, the home of Rolls-Royce. There was no doubt that the coming of the hundredth Japanese company to Britain, hard on the heels of Nissan, Panasonic and Fujitsu would create thousands of new jobs, but equally it raised questions about the inability of Britain's own car industry to compete successfully with the Japanese. Duke (1986), writing from the point of view of an American whose country is also deeply penetrated by Japanese products, suggests that 'Lessons for Industrial America', the subtitle of his book, can be found in *The Japanese School*. Accordingly he highlights various characteristics of Japanese education that have I touched on already in this present volume. Thus his chapter on 'The Loyal Worker' draws on the formative experiences of leadership and cooperation learned in the *han* or the small work group, first created in elementary schools, to which the teacher delegates management powers and responsibilities and which resembles uncannily the quality circles of the Japanese company. Duke's chapters on 'The Literate Worker' and 'The Competent Worker' stress the very high levels of literacy and numeracy that obtain in Japan due to the high priority attached to the three Rs both during and after nine years' compulsory education. Finally, his chapter on 'The Diligent Worker' emphasizes the qualities of effort and perseverance that together produce a nation of people whose striving takes them closer to the limits of their capabilities than would be considered reasonable or possible elsewhere. Duke (1986, p. 186) points out that Japanese companies do not ask any more than this of their schools for they, not the schools, provide the specialized training that their employees need. However, the question naturally arises, if the companies are satisfied with the products of Japanese schools, on what foundations do the schools themselves build in order to produce a nation of loyal, literate, competent and diligent young people? The answer to that question would seem to reside in the way children are brought up in Japan. Hence the aim of this present chapter is to examine child and adolescent development as it is reported by both Japanese and Western writers.

Japanese childhood

The comparative study of childhood in Japan and the West is particularly interesting since, on the one hand, in terms of industrialization, Japan has much in common with the West, yet, on the other hand, with respect to childrearing and education, it has a very distinct cultural tradition of its own. However, the similarities in the one can easily lead to misjudgements about the other, as Azuma (1986, p. 4), who has extensive experience of lecturing in both Japan and the West, makes clear. He gives a familiar enough example of a child refusing to eat a particular dish of food and of a Japanese mother saying: 'All right, then, you don't have to eat it.' The meaning of this sentence seems clear enough to a Western observer since the mother, for whatever reason, is not insisting that the child eat the food and the child is therefore free to leave the dish and quite possibly the table, too. However, this interpretation would be completely wrong, Azuma tells us, for the subtext of the mother's message is in fact a powerful threat along the lines of 'We have been close together. But now that you want to have your own way, I will not care what you do. You are not part of me any longer.' The reason for our failure to spot the covert threat in the Japanese mother's sentence is that we are not privy to the concept of *amae* which suffuses Japanese childrearing practices and which Azuma defines as 'the feeling of dependency coupled with the expectation of indulgence'.

It is, of course, not unknown in the West for parents to indulge or spoil their children and by so doing develop a degree of dependency in the young but the concept of *amae* in Japan is in the first place limited to the particular role of mothers. In White's (1987, p. 21) words: 'the central human relationship in Japanese culture is between mother and child'. Thus, although the father is the formal head of the family and is accorded symbolic respect, his position in reality is marginal for he has little or nothing to do with the bringing up of his children and may be regarded by his wife as little more than an additional, though somewhat less tractable, child. Many Japanese fathers seem happy to collude with this perception of their role since they are after all grown-up children of the *amae* culture which supports the view that 'a good husband is one who is healthy and stays out of the home' (White, 1987, p. 8). Certainly, many Japanese men stay out of the home for most of the day and evening because after work social drinking with colleagues is expected of them and their wives perforce are left to indulge, nurture and care for the children. All too often in today's nuclear families the mother may be the sole caretaker of the children for six days a week, with the result that the mother–child bond is more intense than at any time in the past. In fact, Sunday may be the only day of the week when many fathers see their children awake and for this reason one popular children's book about relationships with one's father is called *My Sunday Friend* (White, 1987, p 108).

Many Western mothers in these circumstances would probably seek to make their children as independent as possible in order to ensure their own survival, but this is not the Japanese way. On the contrary, dependence is encouraged in order that the children may more easily assimilate the hopes and values of their parents. From the beginning the mother makes herself constantly available to her baby and frequently carries or holds the child rather than leave the infant in a cot or playpen. Contact is maintained on shopping expeditions and other outings by carrying the baby on the back rather than pushing it in a pram and at night immediacy of contact is still possible because the baby most frequently sleeps next to or on the mother's futon. Indeed, Hendry (1986, p. 98) reports that 'the Western practice of putting a baby into a cot in another room and leaving it to cry itself to sleep [is] shocking to most Japanese mothers'. However, perhaps the most intimate contact of all, described by the Japanese with an English word 'skinship', is experienced by members of the family and particularly mother and child when they bathe together either at home or in the public bath house. Despite or perhaps because of this prolonged contact between mother and child there is little punishment and much praise in the upbringing of Japanese children. This particular aspect of maternal indulgence has been much commented on by Westerners who have lived in Japan for any length of time. For example, Singleton (1967, p. 10), who lived in 'Nippon City' with his family for ten months, noted how 'the whole family strives to communicate affection for the child' and that 'physical punishment is extremely rare.' He observed that 'a mother or grandmother attempting to dissuade a small boy from some destructive or dangerous action will inevitably say, ''You're a good boy (*oriko*)''. One never hears, ''You're a bad boy,'' or ''Bad boys do that, but good boys don't.'' Similarly, Hendry (1986, p. 100), who spent at least 18 months in Japan with her family, comments on her nextdoor neighbours, from whom she was separated by 'a very thin wall', that she 'never heard the mother raise her voice, either to an often quite miserable baby or to her mischievous four year old'. Again, White (1987, p. 109), who has spent some years in Japan, writes of 'the positive tone that suffuses all the interactions with children' and continues: 'rarely does one hear threats, warnings, or pronouncements, not to speak of character denunciations; nor do teachers or parents confront children directly . . . mothers cajole and persuade through love, not war'.

One substantial reason why children in Japan are constantly treated in such a warm and positive way is the widespread belief that they are inherently good at birth and that there is, therefore, no need to apply strict discipline in order to make them fit for this world. This view stands in direct contrast to the Christian tradition, which has been the dominant ideology in the West for many centuries past and which maintains that man is inherently evil and cannot be otherwise without divine assistance. According to Kojima (1986, p. 42), the Japanese belief in the original goodness of children can be traced back to the Chinese Confucian Mencius (327–289 BC) who thought that 'all evil in human beings is the result of events that corrupt the originally good nature of the child'; but both Azuma (1986, p. 9) and Yamamura (1986, p. 35) seem to have more primitive sources in mind when they quote folk traditions concerning the divine nature of children and the importance of treating them with indulgence and tenderness for fear that they might return to the other world. Whatever the source of these beliefs in the essential purity and innocence of children, they carry with them the corollary that adults are inferior to the young and that the journey from childhood to adulthood constitutes a fall from grace. In Yamamura's (1986, p. 36) words: 'The fundamental nature of the child is perceived to be both different from, and superior to, that of an adult; the transition from childhood to adulthood is considered a step down.' Curiously, this step *down* is marked in Japanese society by the very same milestones which in British society are regarded as the symbols of a step *up* into adult freedom and independence, namely coming of age, getting married and getting a job. If however entry into adulthood and ultimately parenthood is associated with a shift downwards in self-esteem such that children are protected and indulged, then it seems possible that some children will become tyrants and abuse their parents' devotion. That such actions do occur is of great concern to the Japanese, but more commonly the effect of the unconditional love of the *amae* culture is to produce high motivation towards those goals which have the approval of the child's mother. White (1987, p. 22) quotes the case of Sadaharu Oh, a legendary baseball player who ascribed his success on the field to the link between love and success in Japan. He said: '*Amae* warms the heart but it also enables you to work twice as hard, to overcome the siren songs of laziness.'

The Japanese mother, then, through her constant attention to her children is able both to build up an intimate knowledge of their personalities and to intuit their needs and shape their responses. She acts therefore as a model of adult Japanese empathy where it is the responsibility of the receiver of messages rather than the sender to understand what is intended. Indeed, it is positively impolite for a Japanese to express himself or herself too clearly (Azuma, 1986, p. 9). The Japanese mother also teaches her children how to co-operate and how to avoid confrontation both within the special *amae* relationship and in the outside world by constantly rewarding the successes of the young, by backing down when confrontation looms and by implicitly threatening to withdraw affection when the child insists on its own way. Returning to the example of the Japanese mother saying to her child concerning a dish of food, 'All right, then, you don't have to eat it', we now understand that this is a very real threat to the child that if he or she goes its own way then the *amae* relationship will be ruptured.

There is no reason to suppose, however, that Japanese mothers are any more conscious than mothers elsewhere of the particular methods they use in order to bring up their children in a way that is acceptable to the society in which they live. Certainly they do not see their methods as especially manipulative or underhand but simply as those approved by the *seken*, the 'watchful normative presence' (White, 1987, p. 38) of the community, which comprises the opinions of all those who have views on motherhood such as neighbours, family and teachers. It may be, though, that in Japan a mother feels that her reputation depends crucially on her success in bringing up her children because opportunities for success in other areas are so limited. Befu (1986, p. 18) points out that, although about half the workforce in Japan is female and a considerable proportion of these females are mothers, the term 'working mother' tends to denote economic misfortune because 'mothers should stay at home and look after their children unless they have to work'. This expectation, that a mother's place is in the home, explains why, after decades of economic expansion in Japan, the dominant educational ideal for women is still *ryosai kenbo* — good wife, clever mother. Thus women make up nearly 90 per cent of the student population at junior college where they pursue traditional 'women's subjects' such as home economics, education and nursing and where they discover that after graduation the supply of certificated graduates in these areas so much exceeds demand that they will be advised to take clerical jobs in industry until they get married. Opportunities for women in universities, where they comprise less than a quarter of the student body, are progressively fewer the more prestigious the institution but Narumiya (1986, p. 51) thinks that women's expectations are changing and that women are becoming more vocal about their right to increasing social participation and equality of opportunity. However, motherhood is likely to remain the single most important task in the lives of most Japanese women for the remainder of this century and the beginning of the next.

The *ii ko* (good child) represents the ideal to which all mothering is aimed and it is distinctly Japanese in the way that it combines both self-fulfilment and social integration. In other words, individual abilities and qualities are encouraged in children but only in so far as they contribute to the good of society so that the good child becomes the good social child who will maintain harmony in society. This ideal, then, is poles apart from the aggressive Western individualism implied by the statement: 'There is no such thing as society. There are individual men and women and there are families' (Margaret Thatcher, October, 1987). In Japan, by contrast, 'personal performance is seen not only as evidence of *individual* ability, contributing to an identity demonstrated by skills; it is also a way of cementing one's place in the social environment because it provides evidence of moral character and appropriateness to the milieu' (White and LeVine, 1986, p. 56). Therefore the ideal or wished for qualities that go to make up the good Japanese child may sound somewhat strange to Western ears, especially since few admit of simple literal translation into English language and cultural traditions. Thus valued traits that are believed to make the Japanese child a better social person include mildness or gentleness, compliance or the ability to cooperate, and a cluster of characteristics resulting in bright-eyed, active, brisk and smart behaviour. Just one of these terms, *sunao*, usually translated into English as 'obedient', is given a variety of meanings by Japanese mothers and teachers although they may all be summarized in the phrase 'authentic in intent and cooperative in spirit' (White and LeVine, 1986, p. 58). The problem with the translation 'obedient' is that in England it implies an unequal relationship in which the obeyer is subordinated and obliged to give up a degree of self-determination, whereas in Japan *sunao* implies that by working freely with others the self may be positively enhanced. Similarly, the word *yutaka* or empathic may conjure up English qualities such as sensitivity or even passivity, whereas in Japan a more active, vigorous, creative and lively exchange between persons is intended.

A second cluster of traits describes not so much the goal of being the *ii ko* but how to *become* the good child. Thus the characteristics of persistence and endurance, the ability to reflect on one's weaknesses and, of course, the acceptance of dependence and the expectation of indulgence *all* develop through interaction with one's mother and teacher. At the same time the mother or teacher for her part seeks to develop a child's understanding, as we have seen, through a mixture of indulgence and patience. It is immediately apparent that this list of desired characteristics reveals a very different approach to child rearing and training in Japan from the Western pattern and it is therefore hardly surprising that Western writers have sought among these self-same qualities for clues to Japan's economic success. Duke (1986, p. 122), for example, devotes a whole chapter to the effects of the constant call to persevere or *gambare*.

'Gambare!' 'Persevere!' 'Endure!' 'Don't give up!'
Throughout the lifetime of the Japanese they are surrounded, encouraged and motivated by the spirit of gambare. It begins in the home. The school takes it up from the first day the child enters the classroom. It continues through graduation. The company then thrives on it. It engulfs every facet of society. It is employed in work, study, and even at play and leisure. Gambare is integral to being Japanese.

Similarly, White and LeVine (1986, p. 59) confirm that there is a common saying in Japan that 'It's better to make [the child] endure difficulties' for, so the notion goes, without hardship a person will not become mature but will remain self-centered. Young children, of course, are to be spared hardship but older children, it is thought, can do nothing but gain through intensive study for high school entrance examinations. Indeed it is the belief that the endurance of hardship brings virtue that explains to a considerable extent why, despite token

criticisms of the examination system in Japan, it continues to domi-
nate secondary education. Finally, to become a good child one needs to
practise *hansei* or 'self-examination and reflection' (White and
LeVine, 1986, p. 59). *Hansei* operates at both a personal and at a group
level: at the personal level self-criticism is necessary in Japan because
of the cultural avoidance of criticising others; and at the group level,
whether in school or later in a quality control circle, self-criticism
enables members to examine their motivations and methods as well as
the interactions and dynamics of the group. Lewis (1988, p. 168) noted
that 'reflection and self-criticism were . . . frequent parts of the
curriculum' in the 15 first-grade classrooms she observed in Tokyo.
Rohlen (1983, pp. 180–5) reported one remarkable homeroom period
in which a class of 16-year-olds broke up into small groups or *han* and
discussed for over two hours their response to the suspension for one
week of one of their members for smoking. There was much plain
speaking and much emotional release as the group aired openly their
attitudes and behaviour to the missing member, and Rohlen felt that
he gained a rare insight into Japanese emotions that are more commonly concealed behind politeness and reserve.

The *ii ko*, then, is mild and gentle, able to co-operate, bright-eyed
and active but also ready to persist, endure hardship and engage in
self-examination in order to achieve personal and group goals. That
this ideal child is different from its Western counterparts is demonstrated by the problems that Japanese children experience when they
return to Japan after they have been educated in the United Kingdom or
in the United States because of their parents' jobs. First, they have
invariably fallen behind in the gruelling pace set by the Japanese
schools; and second, they have acquired a foreign 'script for success
in school emphasizing independence, explicitness and uniqueness
— quite un-Japanese values' (Azuma, 1986, p. 9). Apparently
the problem of re-entry is not so much academic as cultural. Lost
grades can be recovered without too much difficulty but independence, explicitness and uniqueness, once tasted and enjoyed, are not
easily relinquished in favour of group loyalty. Yet loyalty to the group
is 'one of the predominant traits of the Japanese'. 'It transcends all
layers of society. It is the stuff of "being Japanese"' (Duke, 1986,
p. 25).

Duke (1986), pursuing his theme that lessons for industrial America
are to be found in the Japanese school, devotes a whole chapter to 'The
Loyal Worker'. His thesis is, quite simply, that from the very first day
at elementary school the Japanese child begins a practical course of
training that is designed to lead to an understanding of how group
leadership is exercised and group harmony attained. The group (*kumi*)
appears, at first sight, to be like any English primary school reception
class but in fact it meets for 230 school days every year compared with

an English total of 190 days, and in addition it frequently eats its lunch in the homeroom for the simple reason that most Japanese schools do not possess a central dining room. Schools may, however, have a central kitchen from which members of the *kumi* can collect food and take it to the homeroom for distribution and to which they will return the dishes after the meal has been eaten and thoroughly cleared away. Japanese teachers, unlike many of their counterparts in England who are only too glad to have a lunch break free from their charges, will usually eat with their *kumi* in the homeroom. Thus the *kumi* spends more time together each day and more days together each year with their teacher than their counterparts in the United Kingdom or in the United States and it is not too fanciful to see in this state of affairs a prefiguring of the longer hours that are worked by many Japanese employees and the manner in which many departmental and divisional managers place their desks alongside their staff rather than in an isolated office. The *kumi* in elementary school not only spends more time together than an equivalent class in a Western country but is sometimes taught together in a way that is not common in England today. Duke (1986, p. 29) gives the example of a calligraphy class where every child attempts the same character and an art class where every individual draws the same scene. However, White (1987, p. 119) describes a science class where children, working in pairs, carry out simple experiments, report back their findings to the whole class and finally write individual laboratory-type reports. As she comments, 'science in the Japanese elementary school is taught not through rote learning, but through experience, observation and experiment' (White, 1987, p. 121). In other words, there is no one prescribed way in which the *kumi* may work together because different curriculum subjects suggest different approaches.

The *kumi*, as we have already noted in the previous chapter, is divided into small sub-groups or *han*. Each *han* comprises four to eight pupils who may stay together for several months at a time. The leader or *hancho* is duly elected by the members of the sub-group and becomes in effect both apprentice teacher and trainee manager. In the former role the *hancho* organizes the *han*, encourages its slower members and reports back to the *kumi* on *han* projects, but in the latter role the *hancho* begins to learn how to exercise leadership in the Japanese manner. This means, essentially, leading with due humility and without charisma because in Japan, as the saying goes, 'the stake that protrudes is driven into the ground'. Leadership, Japanese style, aims at achieving harmony in the work group through consensus by means of discussion with individuals and the whole group. By many Western standards, where leaders have a penchant for quick 'top-level' decisions and a distaste for lengthy discussions with the work group, Japanese procedures may seem unnecessarily time-wasting, inefficient and frustrating. But the Japanese have learnt from their mother's knee how to be mild and gentle and how to co-operate with others and, above all, how to persist and to reflect on their weaknesses. Therefore a leader in Japan is able to spend much time and energy in listening to conflicting opinions which, at first, are often couched in the vaguest of terms, until he is able at last to obtain a consensus and more importantly the full support and loyalty of the workgroup. In the West, by contrast, where it is possible for leaders to be out of touch with the views of the workgroup through lack of interest or fear of knowing they may obtain only grudging support and lukewarm loyalty. Normally in Japan, all school children are eventually elected *hancho* and come to understand the importance of group harmony and loyalty, whereas in the West, typically, few children gain experience in leadership at school.

Japanese mothers prepare their children for school and society not least in their perception of their own role. Motherhood is, of course, taken seriously throughout the world, but in the West it has often to compete with other roles such as wife and careerwoman. It is widely accepted that Western women will work out their priorities as between children, partner, career, friends and personal development and that children will not necessarily occupy first place in the mother's world all or even most of the time. However, in Japan the cultural ideal 'is clear-cut and absolute: motherhood comes first. Neglect of one's responsibility as a mother is inexcusable under any circumstances' (Befu, 1986, p. 25). In order to explain the Japanese disposition to fulfil this ideal, Befu coined the term 'role perfectionism', by which he meant the commitment to perform a role to the best of one's ability whatever its status or however difficult it might be. This high level of commitment to a role is, of course, assisted by other cultural ideals that we have noted above such as the need at all times to persevere. Thus, in brief, Befu is claiming that motherhood in Japan is seen as a role to be performed with as much professional commitment as any other and that 'Japanese women take motherhood as seriously as American women take their jobs' (p. 25). Hendry (1986, p. 32) acknowledges that the general view of motherhood in Japan, especially with regard to young children, does imply a full-time professional commitment, but she found that not all women were happy with this state of affairs and that a number felt that too much was being asked of them and that too little time was available to them for themselves.

It does appear that among the many demands on Japanese mothers there is one, teaching children the skills of literacy, that is self-generated. Elementary schools in Japan are perfectly capable of teaching reading and writing skills from scratch but the evidence suggests that most five-year-olds can read at least 60 of the 82 *kana* characters before they start compulsory education (Hendry, 1986, p. 26). It will be remembered that Japanese children have to learn two syllabaries or phonetic 'alphabets' — *hiragana* for Japanese words and *katakana* for borrowed foreign words (e.g., Coca Cola), known collectively as *kana* (Lambert, 1989, p. 12). *Kana* is a syllabic script or 'alphabet' that represents all the basic syllables of the Japanese language; therefore, once a child is competent in *kana* it can read and write every word in its vocabulary. It is true that Japanese children learn to replace, progressively, the simplified *kana* symbols as they advance through the school system by more complex Chinese characters (*kanji*) but the fact remains that most Japanese children can read and write a considerable part of their speaking vocabulary in *kana* before they even begin compulsory school.

That this situation exists at all is due in no small measure to the mothers of Japan, for behind many a Japanese child is a *kyoiku mama* or education mum who will not only make sure her child is well versed in *kana* before entering school but will monitor her child's progress in *kokugo*, the national language, throughout his or her school career. In these circumstances it is perhaps not surprising that nearly all Japanese children are functionally literate at the end of their nine years' state education (Duke, 1986, p. 53). This is not to say that Japanese children do not have reading difficulties — indeed, recent research has shown that 'reading disabilities in Japan are not so rare as has been believed but appear to be as prevalent as in many Western countries' (Hirose and Hatta, 1988, p. 159) — rather that by dint of hard work and perseverance most children are able to read and write by the time they leave school. It is notoriously difficult to define literacy and to measure it at a national let alone an international level (DES, 1975, p. 11), but Japanese superiority in international tests in mathematics and science makes it at least plausible that the frequent claims for Japanese superiority in literacy are well founded.

Japanese children, then, are gifts of the gods who in their early years can do no wrong because they are believed to be inherently good at birth. They are, therefore, loved and indulged by all the family but particularly by their mothers who by this powerful means of shaping behaviour prepare them both for school and society. It is possible to make general statements of this nature about Japanese society with some confidence because it has shown 'great stability over time and great continuity in ideology and values' (White and LeVine, 1986, p. 61). Indeed, this homogeneity of attitudes and beliefs extends to education, where there is great unity of purpose between the goals of parents and teachers and much collaboration between home and school especially at the elementary level. Childhood in Japan, then, is the best of times when indulgence at home is tempered by a growing understanding at the local elementary school of the importance of group loyalty and group harmony.

Japanese adolescence

The comparative study of adolescence in Japan and the West is made interesting from the very beginning by the fact that there is no Japanese-language equivalent for the word 'adolescent' and no cultural tradition for regarding teenagers as a special age group with special problems (White, 1987, p. 152). Thus Rohlen (1983, p. 195) discovered, much to his surprise, that high school teachers in Japan both refer to their students collectively, aged between 15 and 18 years, as *kodomo* or children and customarily treat them as such. In the English and American traditions high school students are regarded, if not as adults, then as people who are to all intents and purposes on the verge of adulthood, but Japanese high school teachers simply do not see their students as approaching maturity but as children who are to be reminded of their duties to family, school and society and who are to be kept away, for as long as possible, from the pleasures and vices of the adult world. In fact, young people in Japan do not reach the age of majority until they are 20 and, as we have seen in Chapter 3, at that age over 50 per cent are still experiencing some form of full-time education.

In effect, adult maturity in Japan is postponed to a considerable degree by formal education, whereas in the West early maturity is generally encouraged with young people's education suffering perhaps as a consequence. As we have seen, over 90 per cent of 17-year-olds in Japan attend upper secondary school, compared with 19 per cent in English schools with an additional 14 per cent in Colleges of Further Education (DES, 1988b). What is more, Japanese young people attend secondary school for six days a week 40 weeks a year and accept levels of control from teachers over standards of dress and behaviour that would be tolerated by very few students in the United Kingdom. As we noted in Chapter 3, school rules extend far beyond the school gates and teachers are expected to reprimand pupils discovered smoking, drinking or riding motorcycles wherever they might be. Schools also vet students' part-time or vacation jobs since out-of-school work might interfere with vital preparation for college entrance examinations or, even worse, introduce students too soon to corrupting elements in adult life. Yet, despite what many Western adolescents would regard as intolerable interference with their freedom, the vast majority of Japanese young people cheerfully accept the requirements of their school and treat their teachers with deference and respect. One recent report (Hewitt and Takayama, 1988) does describe a rally in Tokyo attended by lawyers, parents and students at which passionate protests were made against school rules or *kosoku* that date from the late nineteenth century and that might well violate basic human rights, but the same report recognizes that outbursts against regimentation in

Japanese schools, however sincere, stand little chance of popular support because of the widespread fear that without *kosoku*, order and harmony in schools would break down and would be replaced by Western-style indiscipline and misbehaviour.

One further reason for the widespread acquiescence of Japanese young people in the values of their school is that in Japan there is no developed youth culture which is at odds with the aims of education. At root this is because, by Western standards, Japanese adolescent social life is considerably underdeveloped. This is not to say that friendships with peers are not important or that the young are not fashion-conscious or even that adolescents do not entertain romantic dreams, rather that *opportunities* for developing these aspects of social life are many fewer than in the West. For example, same-sex friends are largely made at school and, during the years of compulsory education, are likely to live in the neighbourhood surrounding the school; but with the transition from junior to senior high school, established friendship patterns are often broken up and students are obliged to seek new friends. Boys are often less successful than girls in this search, with up to a third lacking a close friend at high school (Rohlen, 1983, p. 285). Furthermore, high school students often commute to school and may therefore live some considerable distance from their new friends. Visits may be arranged but, even so, most Japanese homes do not have rooms where young people can be alone. Friendship groups, gangs or cliques are therefore comparatively rare among Japanese teen-agers because there are few social gatherings where students can meet outside supervised educational clubs and classes. Therefore, same-sex friendships tend to be close and long-lasting since opportunities for making new friends are strictly limited and opposite-sex friendships in the Western sense are very much the exception rather than the rule. In a 1977 survey, over 50 per cent of high school students said they did not have a friend of the opposite sex, although 7 per cent claimed to have a lover or *koibito* (Rohlen, 1983, p. 288). However, in Japan it is perfectly possible for young lovers to have few, if any, evening 'dates' and to limit the expression of their love to holding hands. So by Western standards Japanese young people seem modest and naïve in the extreme, but by Japanese standards some Western adolescents seem shocking and primitive in their unabashed displays of sexuality. This is not to say that the Japanese are puritanical about sex, far from it, but that they value propriety and status a great deal and consider the deferment of romantic activity until after college entrance has been secured an entirely appropriate behaviour for school children.

However, about 40 per cent of young people in Japan enter the labour market rather than college at the age of 18 and it is they rather than their academic peers who may have experienced a less restricted adolescence. For example, they are more likely to have attended vocational schools or low-status private schools, to have had part-time and summer vacation jobs, to have done less homework, hung around in groups after school, ridden motorcycles, played truant or engaged in delinquent behaviour. The most common form of delinquency, theft, may arise because some students from low- rather than high-status schools possess lower levels of academic motivation, experience less parental supervision and have more opportunity to spend time on the streets at weekends and after school. Certainly Rohlen (1983, p. 298) found that in Kobe the police were more likely to arrest or warn students from schools that were ranked low rather than high in public esteem, but his observation that 'delinquency is obviously correlated with school rank' is unlikely to surprise many Western readers although they might well envy the Japanese their relatively low levels of juvenile crime. What, however, has caused consternation in Japan and some surprise in the West is the growing number of incidents involving violence towards teachers in junior high schools.

The number of assaults on Japanese teachers doubled in the late 1970s but appeared to peak in 1982 (Reeves, 1985, p. 24). In that year 1,123 junior high school teachers were assaulted, according to police records, compared with 39 senior high school staff. Given that there were about 278,900 lower secondary school teachers, both public and private, in May 1984 (Leestma *et al.*, 1987, p. 79), it would appear that on average about one junior high school teacher in 250 was in danger of physical assault during that year. In England, according to a recent report on discipline in schools (DES, 1989c, p. 230), it was estimated that one secondary teacher in 200 had been subjected to an incident 'of a clearly violent nature' during *one week* in October 1988. Since the English statistics were not taken from police records but from questionnaires completed in about 250 secondary schools and since 'most local education authorities do not appear to keep any systematic record of serious incidents in schools' (DES, 1989c, p. 189), direct comparisons with Japan are not easy to make but there does seem to be a prima facie case for suggesting that a much higher level of violent activity exists in English schools. Some British press reaction to the Elton report on discipline in schools was, however, distinctly muted, with headlines such as 'violence rare, teachers say' (*The Guardian*, 14 March 1989), whereas in Japan public response to violence in the home and in schools has been considerable. According to Nishimura (1985, p. 19), who writes articles on education and social issues for the *Asahi Shimbun*, a leading national newspaper, what has shocked the Japanese public is that attacks on teachers violate 'the most fundamental code of Confucian-influenced traditional educational values — namely, respecting and obeying teachers'. Nishimura, like many other Japanese observers, locates the root cause of the breaching of these values in the intense pressures to which junior high school students are subjected in their efforts to gain a crucial foothold on the ladder that leads to university education, and he suggests that educational reform, the subject of the final chapter of this book, is one way in which these pressures might be eased.

However, it is noticeable that some contemporary descriptions of adolescence in Japan are beginning to resemble outmoded Western concepts of adolescent development which saw it as a time of emotional turmoil. For example, Kashiwagi (1986, p. 164) in introducing the only chapter on adolescence in the book *Child Development and Education in Japan* (Stevenson *et al.*, 1986), notes that there are two serious problems for Japanese adolescents: first, the pressures in their lives to succeed in entrance examinations; and second, the increase in juvenile delinquency particularly in the junior high school period. What she does not point out, however, is that although nearly all adolescents in Japan experience *juken jigoku* (examination hell) in junior high school, only a tiny minority engage in delinquent behaviour. Hence her approach runs the risk of tarring all young people with the same brush in much the same way as the classical psychoanalytic position in the West — which affirms that storm and stress is a *normal* condition of all adolescents — fails to recognize that 'most young people go through their teenage years without significant emotional or behavioural problems' (Rutter, 1979, p. 86). Rutter, who has done much to disseminate a balanced view of adolescent development, draws on his own and many other large-scale surveys of randomly selected populations of young people to make clear that it is unwise of psychiatrists and psychologists to make general statements about all young people on the basis of their interviews with selected client populations in clinics and hospitals. Similarly, it is important when discussing adolescence in Japan, particularly at the lower secondary school level, not to dwell on the distressing behaviour of the few to the exclusion of a consideration of the views of the majority.

In 1986 I was able to carry out a study at two junior high schools in Japan, one in the Chiba prefecture of the Kanto district not far from Tokyo and the other in the Wakayama prefecture of Kinki district about 120 kilometres due south of Osaka. The study involved 283 ninth-grade (14-year-old) pupils whose responses I compared with those of a larger study conducted in England in 1981 at six schools in the Midlands where the entire fourth year or tenth grade of each school took part (Simmons and Wade, 1984). The aim of both surveys was to discover what a representative sample of young people thought, felt and believed about important aspects of their lives, using as evidence their own written statements. The statements were made in response to ten unfinished sentences in an open-ended questionnaire, which for the purposes of the comparative study was translated into Japanese.

For interested readers the questionnaire can be found in the appendix together with a statistical analysis of the main findings. What follows here is an account of the main *themes* that could be identified from the written responses of the two groups of young people.

In response to the first sentence about their *ideal person*, 19 per cent of the English wrote that they did not wish to be like anyone else. One boy wrote: 'I can't think of somebody I would like to be like. After all what is wrong with being yourself?' In the past this might have been considered a cheeky or even a defensive response, but nowadays it is more usual to regard it as an indicator of a healthy and confident individuality. In Japan, however, such an unambiguous declaration of selfhood would normally be considered impolite and in fact only one boy in the Japanese survey made such a response, 'myself, now', although it was clear from the rest of his paper that he regarded himself as something of a rebel who was impatient with the social and language conventions of his time. In response to the second sentence concerning their *least ideal person*, 10 per cent of the English wrote that they would least like to be like *politicians* and 50 individuals (6 per cent) specifically named the Prime Minister, Margaret Thatcher. By contrast, only three Japanese referred to politicians, although one boy did express himself strongly on the point: 'Politicians. No matter how many good things they promise they are probably wangling something in the background. I detest politicians who are like wolves in sheep's clothing.' It would appear, then, that English young people are more politically aware than their Japanese counterparts, although the English survey in 1981 took place at a time when the British Prime Minister's popularity was at a very low ebb and when she was constantly in the news. Unemployment was rising sharply, riots were shortly to take place in several cities, most notably in Brixton (London) and Toxteth (Liverpool); and the Falklands War, which was to do so much to restore her popularity, was yet to be fought and won. By contrast the Japanese survey took place in 1986, three years before Prime Minister Takeshita was forced to resign over the Recruit share scandal. However, an earlier English survey (Edwards, 1973) recorded 36 per cent of a sample of 15-year-olds nominating politicians as least liked persons, and it is possible that the English, with their patterns of early school leaving and early expectations of adulthood, take a more lively interest in political matters than their Japanese counterparts, especially when high-profile prime ministers like Margaret Thatcher are in office.

In response to the third sentence concerning *preferred companions*, about half the young people in both surveys nominated their *friends*. In both countries the schools provide opportunities for consolidating friendships over a number of years, but in Japan transfers to high schools break up established friendship patterns at 15 years of age, while in England transfers to sixth form, further education, Youth Training Schemes, employment or unemployment have a similar effect on 16-year-olds. In both countries, then, a roughly equal proportion of teenagers value the companionship of their peers but the proportion valuing their parents differs significantly. In the English survey 39 per cent nominated the *family*, which usually means parents, as the people with whom they were happiest, and many youngsters spoke eloquently of the importance to them of family life. For example, one girl wrote that she is happiest with

> my family, my mother, sisters, Aunties, Uncles and my Grandad. They make life seem worth living some days and give you courage to go on and succeed. They give me a kind of drive and an aim. Most of all they make you happy when things are down. I have a crippled Auntie and whenever I feel sorry for myself I think of her, for she is always happy.

In the Japanese study, by contrast, only 16 per cent cited the family as preferred companions, although a number were very positive in their comments. One boy wrote that the people he was happiest with are 'the six members in my family. Family circles are good', and one girl wrote at greater length and intensity: 'Family. No matter what I say I think the people who understand me the best are my parents. Also I think that the people who worry about me 10 times more, 100 times more than anyone else are my parents.' This girl seems to be in the habit of saying one thing about her family, which may be critical, while actually thinking and writing another which is much more favourable, but in fact in the surveys neither the English nor the Japanese were very critical about their families for only 6 per cent of the former and 3 per cent of the latter nominated them as *least preferred companions* in response to the fourth sentence. Indeed, in both countries it is *teachers* who are slightly ahead of families as least desired people! However, the low level of positive reference by Japanese young people to their parents is puzzling.

In English the meaning of the sixth sentence is unambiguous — it refers to what is of *supreme importance* to the respondent — but in the Japanese translation it can also mean, as one of the participants pointed out, *the most serious thing* for me. It is possible that this ambiguity of meaning contributed something to the major differences between the two surveys at this point, for in England the *family* was of supreme importance to 32 per cent, *friends* to 22 per cent, and *getting a job* to 14 per cent; whereas in Japan the number of nominations for *friends* was similar to the English but only 5 per cent nominated their *parents* and a mere 3 per cent cited *getting a job*. A possible explanation for this second significant difference between the two surveys with regard to nominations for parents may lie in the themes that dominated the Japanese responses to the sixth sentence. These were *studying* (21 per cent) and *entering high school* (15 per cent), with an extra 5 per cent citing *exams* alone. The following quotations sum up very well what is of supreme importance to 14-year-old Japanese children approaching their first experience of *juken jigoku*: 'At the moment there is only one thing: studying for exams.' 'Entering the prefectural high school and progressing to my favourite university.' 'My future is decided by exams so I must try hard'. One girl writes at greater length than most and puts studying into a life-long perspective, while at the same time placing self-development in the crucial Japanese context of social relationships. Her thoughts are such that it would be difficult to imagine an English 14-year-old writing in the same vein and placing so much emphasis on study. What matters most, then, to one Japanese girl is:

> At this point in time studying. Also, for my whole life, things which I think are important to me are discovering myself and my relationship in society. And I will never forget the final words of a teacher when he retired from my high school last year: 'Life, until death, is study.'

However, it is not only in the sixth sentence that differences in priorities can be seen between the English and the Japanese respondents. In completing sentence seven, 22 per cent of the Japanese made it clear that *entering high school* or *passing high school entrance examinations* would be the *best possible outcome* for them. Indeed, one girl clearly recognized that the entrance examinations were a particular characteristic of Japan, therefore the best thing that could happen to her was 'passing the high school entrance exams because I don't think there are many students in countries other than Japan who are pushed into high school entrance so I think that passing the exams is the best thing that could happen to me'. It would seem that this girl takes some pride, however circular her argument, in the challenge of *juken senso* (examination war) and it is quite possible that she speaks for others. Certainly an even greater number of Japanese in the survey (25 per cent) in response to the eighth sentence, wrote that the *worst outcome* in their present lives would be to *fail high school entrance examinations*. One girl notes that the worst thing that could happen to her would be 'failing all the entrance examinations to all the high schools which I have tried for', thus revealing a very different set of preoccupations from those of her English counterparts. In 1981, the year of the English survey, the level of unemployment rose to well over 2 million people, eight years later it was still nearly 2 million despite numerous changes in the methods of collecting the statistics in the intervening years. Against this background it is not surprising that 27 per cent of English 15-year-olds, in response to the seventh sentence, were of the opinion that the *best possible outcome* for them would be *to get a job*. Jobs take over from schools as organizers of time and providers of goals and new sets of relationships in the adult world, and so, for many adolescents in England, getting a job is synonymous with becoming a fully fledged adult (Hargreaves, 1981). Interestingly, a Japanese boy responding to the ninth sentence agrees with this view. 'The best thing about life', he writes, 'is finding employment because you'll become a member of society.' My translators pointed out to me in a letter that 'there is a special word for "member of society" and that you are not considered to be a member until you have completed your education and have got a job'. In Japan less than 1 per cent of 16-year-olds are unemployed; in England 7 per cent are, with a further 24 per cent on Youth Training Schemes.

Further *desired outcomes* in response to the seventh sentence in the English survey were *passing exams* and *winning the pools* (both at 18 per cent). The first was often seen as a necessary preliminary to getting a job rather than an entrance examination to higher levels of education, and the second as a fantastic alternative to work comparable with winning the lottery in Japan. Two of the themes from sentence seven (*employment* and *passing exams*) were mirrored in the English survey in sentence eight (*unemployment* and *failing* exams, both at 13 per cent), but three new themes emerged as more greatly *feared* outcomes to life — *death* (16 per cent), *personal disablement* as a result of an accident (20 per cent) and the *death of relatives* (23 per cent). One girl wrote simply that the worst thing that could happen 'is that my parents died'. For the Japanese, however, their *own death* (20 per cent) is a more feared outcome than the *death of their parents* (7 per cent). Once again, as in sentences three and six, it is not easy to interpret this low level of reference to and apparent low regard for Japanese parents by their children. Certainly there are no frank avowals of regard for parents in the Japanese survey that equal the responses of many of the English teenagers. For example, one English girl wrote in response to sentence eight concerning the blow that the death of her parents would cause her: 'They are the most important people in my life at my age and to lose them would be the worst thing that could happen. This is because I have such a great relationship with them.'

It might be that modesty restrains the Japanese more than the English in confessing their love for their parents or, as it was suggested to me in discussions in Tokyo, that Japanese children simply take their parents' love for granted and do not need to state the obvious; or it may be that the enormous pressures on the young to succeed at school in Japan have taken their toll on family life and have made home seem less a place of refuge and relaxation and more an extension of school. Certainly one of the arguments currently used against reducing the

Japanese school week from six to five days is that it would make more time available for children to study at home and attend *juku* (Duke, 1986, p. 212). Again, in Lynn's (1988, p. 2) words, public concern about education in Japan is that it is 'too competitive and that children are working too hard at the expense of their social and cultural development'. Some evidence for this statement can be found in the responses to the fifth sentence.

This sentence, which is concerned with the use of free time and private leisure, reveals that around one-third of both groups of young people *read* when they are by themselves as well as *listen to music* on radio, records and tapes. Doubtless some of the reading matter in both countries is not very demanding but in Japan the comic books or *manga* have to be seen to be believed. They can be up to 350 pages long and are 'nearly wordless and full of violence' (White, 1987, p. 154). They are widely available for sale and can be found in may cafés and restaurants. White thinks that a typical high school student may read two or three *manga* a week, but I have no information on the reading habits of junior high school students. Significantly, more Japanese (43 per cent) than English (28 per cent) wrote that they *watched TV* when they were by themselves, possibly because many more English than Japanese teenagers lead an active social life outside the home and would regard watching TV by themselves as a lonely and unwanted experience. Two themes, however, that featured in the Japanese survey but not in the English were *studying* (9 per cent) and *sleep* (19 per cent). In Japan the two activities are not unconnected, as the variously reported saying about examinations and sleep, 'Pass with four, fail with five', indicates. It may well be that if sleep is such a precious resource for Japanese teenagers that they value it more highly than their English counterparts as a final escape from the pressing demands of study.

Sentences nine and ten, by inviting young people to contemplate what they regard as the *best* and *worst aspects of their lives*, necessarily involve them in expressing a small part of their personal philosophy. In the English survey hedonism topped the list, with 17 per cent citing *enjoyment* as the best thing about life followed by numerous statements (15 per cent) concerning the role of *friends* in contributing to one's happiness. One English girl, for example, wrote that 'Life is what you make it. The social life, the laughs and possibly the funny moments of crying. The shyness and joys of having boyfriends and girlfriends.' As we have seen before, few Japanese young people are able to enjoy a mixed social life of the English variety, and so it is to *marriage* that 17 per cent in the Japanese survey look forward. One girl writes that the best thing about life 'is encountering a nice person and getting married . . . because I'd hate it if I got divorced and I think my parents would be very upset'. In fact this 14-year-old girl is likely to wait at least ten years for her wedding, since marriage occurs, on average, later in Japan than in any other developed nation and, even when it does occur, it is quite possible that this girl may have had no serious romantic affairs, even with her future spouse (Rohlen, 1983, p. 288). However, life has not always been so in Japan and the most likely cause of today's delays in courtship and marriage is post-war prosperity coupled with a widespread desire for higher education. Nevertheless, divorce rates in Japan are among the lowest in the industrial world (Smith, 1983, p. 120), so the girl quoted above is less likely to experience a broken marriage than her opposite numbers in England, where one in three couples who get married can also expect to be divorced.

Different patterns of adolescent social life leading to different patterns of marriage may well explain the differing ways in which young people in the two surveys responded to sentence nine. As we have seen, *enjoyment* and *friendship* were rated highly by the English as among the best things of life but *marriage* (2 per cent) hardly at all. By contrast, the Japanese rated *marriage* highly (17 per cent) but *living* even more so (28 per cent). For example, one Japanese boy wrote that the best thing about life is 'Living, fully day by day living happily for the present'. A somewhat smaller proportion of the English (11 per cent) thought that *living*, apart from *enjoyment* and *friendship*, was the best thing about life but then, in response to sentence ten, a smaller proportion of the English (21 per cent) than the Japanese (40 per cent) thought that the worst thing about life was *death*. At one level death or dying seems an obvious enough completion of sentence ten, as in the following response of a Japanese boy 'The worst thing about life is dying because if you die that's an end of everything'; but at another level the responses to sentence ten are as revealing of cultural differences as the material generated by any other sentence. Thus, no English response could match that of the Japanese boy who wrote that the worst thing about life is 'passing away with regret because I believe that if I die in remorse my soul will remain in the world feeling bitter and vexed'. English 15-year-olds, by contrast, are more likely to express their regrets in this life than to imagine taking them to the world to come; chief among these regrets are *school* (13 per cent) and *violence* (10 per cent). An English girl graphically expresses her dislike of education in terms that do not surface in the Japanese survey: 'school every bloody day, day after day, for eleven years or more'; and a compatriot writes of violence in language that would not occur to a Japanese girl: 'The terrible things that happen eg. murder, rape, theft. It is horrible not being able to walk anywhere without the fear of being attacked. We say that we have a Free country but we do not really.' Thus this comparative survey reminds us at the very end that attitudes to education in Japan are more positive, or at least less negative, than in England and that crime rates are very much lower. But it also reminds us that, of the two 'serious problems for Japanese adolescents' (Kashiwagi, 1986, p. 167) noted earlier only the first, examination pressures, has emerged as a major theme in this study. The second, the increase in juvenile delinquency, particularly among those of junior high school age, failed to surface and indeed it is the adult delinquency of *war* which the Japanese young people, in much the same proportion as the English (around 10 per cent), see as the worst thing about life.

The dominant *themes* that have been discussed above were easily identified in the responses of the two groups of young people to the open-ended questionnaire and had only to be totalled, whereas the dominant *values* expressed in the comparative study had to be allotted according to a six-point scale devised originally by Havighurst and Taba (1949). Examples from all six categories ranging from materialistic to altruistic responses are given below, the first five in response to sentence one and the sixth to sentence six. All are taken from the Japanese survey.

Materialistic — Category 0
> I want to be a rich man.
> I want to get my driver's licence for motorcycles and cars.   Male

Physical Appearance and Popularity — Category 1
> the best type is a person with beautiful hair, a pretty face, a person who is gentle and kind to anyone, who studies well, is tall, cooks well and can cook things which we can't cook. Also the best type is bust 8, waist 5, hip 8.   Female

Friendly, Courteous, Good-humoured — Category 2
> A person who is kind to the elderly, who gets on well with friends and uses honorific language to superior people.   Male

Honest, Reliable, Industrious, Kind — Category 3
> a person who thinks of other people not only himself (a person who is kind to others)   Female

Co-operative and Helpful — Category 4
> A person who can do anything for others and is obedient and bright. A person who can value others. A person who helps others without being told to. Because I want to be able to value others.   Female

Social Justice and Human Brotherhood — Category 5
> Preserving peace in the world. It's better to have a big dream.   Male

In the English study there were striking differences between the *values* expressed by the two sexes, therefore we know with a considerable degree of certainty that English girls, more than boys, tend to hold beliefs that are less materialistic and more to do with inter-personal relationships. Thus girls are more likely than boys to write 'I would like to get on with people better — and to help others'; and boys are more likely than girls to write 'I would love to be rich and have a big car' or 'I would like a job in which I could order people about'.

In the Japanese study similar differences were found and for similar reasons but not to the same degree. It would seem, therefore, that Japanese males and females are generally closer in their valuing than their English counterparts, while at the same time being significantly different from the English. In other words, the English males in the comparative survey were the most likely group to make materialistic responses and the least likely to make responses to do with inter-personal relationships, while the Japanese females were the group least likely to respond in the manner of the English males. For the statistically minded a summary of the analysis of the values expressed in the two surveys can be found in Table 2 at the end of this book together with a discussion of the statistical method used.

Japanese adolescence, then, like Japanese childhood, is very different from the English experience. It is dominated for the most part by educational aspirations which serve to prolong the age of childhood and to ensure a more home-based and study-centred life than that of many English young people, who prefer the society of friends, both male and female, and the freedoms of early adulthood. In Japan there is no word for 'adolescence' and no concept for that part of life which is frequently characterized in the West as a special period with special problems. However, a rise in the 1980s of school violence, particularly in the junior high school age group, has led one Japanese writer at least to adopt some of the terms and images utilized by Western psychologists in discussing adolescence. Nevertheless, the abiding hallmark of adolescence in Japan is one of a period of life that is devoted more to education than in any other nation of the world and that the zeal for educational attainment displayed by the young during this period might well be the root cause of their nation's economic might.

5

Educational reform

From time to time in this book parallels have been drawn between the
English and the Japanese educational systems, but the case for doing so
in this final chapter is particularly compelling since major educational
reforms occurred in both countries at similar times and for related
reasons. Thus in 1872 in Japan universal popular elementary education was established at the beginning of the reign of the Emperor
Meiji to replace the classical Chinese education of the Tokugawa
era and to bring about a programme of rapid modernization, Westernization and industrialization. In 1947 popular secondary education
began as a result of the United States forces of occupation under
General MacArthur ordering the reform of the elitist, nationalistic
and militaristic system that they discovered in 1945, in the light of
American ideals of democratic and comprehensive education. But in
1984 Prime Minister Yasuhiro Nakasone, for political as much as
educational reasons, established an *ad hoc* Council on Education
under Michio Okamoto, a former president of Kyoto University, to
review the post-war system and to draft plans for a third major
reform of education in Japan. The Prime Minister's action constituted
a considerable personal initiative and a break with tradition in that the
normal organ for considering educational measures in Japan, the
Central Council on Education, was suspended for three years on the
grounds that it would not come up with sufficiently radical solutions
to deal with the educational problems facing Japan in the 1980s. In
August 1987 the renamed National Council for Educational Reform,
no longer *ad hoc* but national in scope and reforming in purpose, published the results of its deliberations in *The Fourth and Final Report of
Educational Reform* (Government of Japan, 1987). The four reports
were deeply critical of contemporary Japanese education for being narrow in outlook, uniform and outmoded in delivery, slow to change and
out of touch with the needs of society; but the reality of that society

was that once Yasuhiro Nakasone was no longer Prime Minister the political will to bring about the changes recommended in the reports largely departed, and it is unlikely that radical reform will take place in the immediate future (Cantor, 1989, p. 11).

In the United Kingdom, a similar pattern of reform acts can be observed. Thus in 1870 universal popular elementary education was established in England and Wales in the first of many attempts to educate the workforce in order to maintain Britain's position in the industrial world in the face of increasing foreign competition. By the end of the nineteenth century attendance levels at British elementary schools were ahead of those for Japanese schools; indeed, the new 'board' schools were proving so popular with working-class pupils that in some of our cities and large towns new forms of vocational education with a scientific and technological bias were developing for those who wished to continue their education beyond the age of 12. However, in the first part of the twentieth century levels of attendance at elementary schools in Japan came to equal our own and, as we have seen, in addition to the elite middle schools for academically able males, vocational education was developed and became a significant force in secondary education. In England and Wales, by contrast, the literary and non-vocational elite grammar schools for both sexes became the only substantial route for secondary education and the vocational, technical and scientific route was severely curtailed though not entirely cut off. As a result of these differing national priorities the Japanese had in position in 1941 a form of tripartite education that ensured that most of their children remained in school, even if only on a part-time basis, until the age of 17; while in England and Wales secondary education for all did not become a national priority until the passing of the 'Butler' Education Act of 1944.

The ideal of the 1944 Act that there should be parity of esteem between grammar schools and the new secondary modern schools was never realized because the grammar schools continued and in greatly reduced numbers still continue, to be regarded by many as elite institutions, whereas the secondary modern schools were seen from the start as inferior because their pupils, by definition, had 'failed' their grammar school entrance examinations. Consequently the next four decades in England and Wales were taken up with attempts to bring about a more egalitarian education service by establishing a system of comprehensive schools with, eventually, a comprehensive examination at 16. As a result, by the late 1980s around 90 per cent of children in England and Wales attended comprehensive schools and were entered for the General Certificate of Secondary Education. In Japan, by contrast, the intervention of the Americans in 1945 in their post-war educational plans meant that comprehensive education was established in 1947 for nearly all children and that examinations

taken at the age of 15 became *entrance* examinations for upper secondary schools rather than school *leaving* examinations after the English
pattern. However, in 1987, at the same time as the National Council
for Education Reform in Japan was preparing its fourth and final report,
a British Cabinet committee was meeting in secret and in splendid
isolation from educationalists to prepare a radical programme for
educational reform to be launched in the Conservative Party mani-
festo for the general election of 1987 (Maclure, 1988, p. 166).

In the event the Conservative Party won the general election and in
little over a year the Education Reform Act was on the statute book. By
British standards the new act was a radical one that was certain to
bring about fundamental change, and yet many of its more controversial sections were familiar enough to the Japanese. For example, despite ritual denials by Kenneth Baker, the then Secretary of State for
Education and Science, that the Act was *not* about 'enhancing central
control' (Maclure, 1988, p. xii), his powers and those of his department *were* greatly increased by the new legislation. But in Japan the
French model of a centralized education system had been adopted from
the very beginning in 1872. It is true there was an enforced flirtation
with the American model of decentralization through elected, independent local boards, as noted in Chapter 3, but since the mid-
1950s there has been a consistent tendency for central government to regain its former powers 'over the whole area of the nation's
education' (Kobayashi, 1976, p. 85). Both Japanese and British conservative governments have similar reasons for liking central control, for
it means that those who oppose their views, on Japanese local boards or
in British Local Education Authorities, can be outflanked and that
'producer capture' — the tendency of public planning institutions to
act in the interests of those who work for them, the teachers, rather
than those who use their services, the parents and their children —
can be attacked (Morrell, 1989, p. 78). Needless to say, in both countries there have been fierce skirmishes between central and local
government and between ministers of education and teachers' unions,
but in the short term at least those who oppose centralizing tendencies
have been eclipsed. However, there is one section of the English
Reform Act where central direction is no longer regarded as controversial and that is the National Curriculum. The National Curriculum
began to take effect in 1989 and, in Maclure's (1988, p. 9) apt words, it
'provides the local authority, the governors and the head teacher with
their marching orders. A school which is implementing the national
curriculum is working within the law.' In Japan, however, this English
'reform' simply represents normal practice because 'the basic framework for school curricula including the objectives and standard teaching content in each subject is outlined in the "Course of Study" issued
by the Ministry for each of the three school levels' (NIER, 1988, p. 24).

These courses of study are revised about every ten years and those in current use in elementary schools (1980), lower secondary schools (1981) and upper secondary schools (1982) are now due for their next revision. In England and Wales the powers which the Secretary of State has assumed in order to prescribe the curriculum are not in fact new since similar powers existed under the 1902 'Balfour' Act; but curiously, at the same time, in the 1920s, as the Japanese government increased its hold on the curriculum the British government relaxed its control, and at the same time, in the 1940s, as the Americans attempted to decentralize power over the curriculum in Japan the British government gave substantial administrative power to the local education authorities. Only belatedly in England and Wales has central control been reasserted. But even in the Educational Reform Act of 1988 the recommendations of the National Curriculum apply only to pupils from 5 to 16 and not to 18. In Japan, where over 90 per cent of the latter age group attended school throughout the 1980s, such neglect of talent must seem inexplicable.

Another aspect of the Education Reform Act that was seen as controversial was the assessment and testing of pupils at the key stages of 7, 11, 14 and 16. The first assessments in English, mathematics and science will be carried out in 1991 on seven-year-olds, and from 1922 parents will be informed of the results. Results in the older age groups will be published in aggregate form in order to make schools more accountable and to provide parents with more information about their children's progress. The Japanese, of course, are no strangers to assessment and testing, for *juken jigoku* (examination hell) begins to bite in the lower secondary schools and rises to a climax in the upper secondary schools with university entrance examinations. Indeed, interest in the publication of the results of university entrance examinations in Japan amounts to a 'national obsession' (Rohlen, 1983, p. 77) and leads to the most detailed ranking in the national and local press of the feeder high schools according to their successes or failures in placing students in the best universities. It follows that one of the dangers of excessive assessment in schools and of competition between schools is that children are taught to pass tests and little else and that lively and stimulating teaching is replaced by a mechanical drilling of 'facts'. Such teaching has been commonplace in secondary schools in Japan but in England and Wales, to guard against this outcome, the Task Group on Assessment and Testing (TGAT), under Professor Paul Black, has recommended a system that is closely linked to normal classroom assignments and need not therefore operate in opposition to normal processes of learning and teaching. However, only time will tell if these humane recommendations can be followed and the excesses of the Japanese system avoided.

Time, again, will be the chief arbiter of the success of the measures in the Education Act which are aimed at injecting more businesslike attitudes into schools and freeing them from the apron strings of Local Education Authority bureaucracy. These measures did not mean, of course, that significant new moneys would be found for schools, rather that existing moneys would be distributed differently. Thus in 1989 in secondary schools and larger primary schools the governing bodies were made responsible for controlling the budgets delegated to them by the Local Education Authorities and, in addition, a new category of 'grant maintained' school came into being that had voted to 'opt out' of Local Education Authority control altogether in favour of a direct grant from central government. In this latter case the foundation governors are responsible for controlling the finances of a new breed of 'free schools, paid for out of public funds' (Maclure, 1988, p. 56). Finally, the Education Reform Act gave statutory backing to a limited number of independent schools or City Technology Colleges that are sponsored by business and industry, free to users and supported directly by the government with grants and capital payments. In total these various measures are designed to release new entrepreneurial powers in school administrators and governing bodies and to break the monopoly of the Local Education Authorities over state education, but few would doubt that behind these aims lie the seeds of others that will germinate as soon as the climate permits. Chief among these aims will be the desire steadily to reduce, in real terms, the expenditure of central government on state education while, at the same time, increasing opportunities for sponsored and private education. As a result greater differentiation than ever before will become apparent in English education and the relative wealth of parents will increasingly determine the quality of their children's education.

In Japan, as we have seen in Chapter 3, entrepreneurial activity in education exists on a much larger scale than in the United Kingdom but by and large it is separate from the state sector and has come about more through public demand than government legislation. For example, private education in Japan is extremely rare for children up to the age of 15 because government provision for compulsory education is of such a high quality. Nevertheless the post-war years have seen a remarkable flowering of commercially-run crammers (*juku*) for the very same age group. *Juku* receive no government subsidy but they do attract parents in large numbers who are anxious to maximize their children's educational performance. Thus *juku* by their popularity and commercial success, make manifest the high levels of educational motivation and the widespread desire for academic achievement that exist in Japan. Indeed, this same commitment to educational achievement, coupled with a willingness to pay for private education, is also evident at post-compulsory levels in Japan. It is true that government high schools, colleges and universities are usually preferred by the Japanese because of their better facilities and lower fees, but this is not invariably so. The rise of Nada and other successful private second-ary schools has opened up a new route to the elite universities for bright and well-off secondary school students, but it is feared by some that the true cost of this new route will be the weakening of the meritocratic principle which has hitherto been so powerfully present in Japanese education (Rohlen, 1983, p. 313). Indeed, Rohlen believes that 'to the degree that élite education is tied to money, educational opportunity is distorted, and the legitimating power of the merit prin-ciple declines'. In the United Kingdom elite education has always been tied to money, some honourable exceptions apart, and present reforms are likely to increase that tendency, not least because the pursuit of equality of opportunity in the post-war years is deemed by right-wing educationalists to have failed (Morrell, 1989, p. 25). However, it would be ironic in the extreme if the reforms in the English Act of 1988 that largely resemble common practice in Japan should fall at the first hurdle because the merit principle in British education, already weaker than in Japan, should be further undermined by the financial sections of the Reform Act. But there are other indications that the Education Reform Act is built on shifting foundations.

The failure of the British to educate the majority of their young people beyond the age of 16 to a high level of competence has been noted more than once in this book. It comes as no surprise, therefore, that a recent report by the Confederation of British Industry (CBI, 1989) confirms that the percentage of 17-year-olds in full-time education in the United Kingdom is significantly lower than in those nations that are our major competitors and is *less than half the average* for the 23 nations of the Organization for Economic Cooperation and Development (OECD). This waste of British tal-ent, quite apart from its implications for the effectiveness of British industry, also threatens to undermine the foundations of the Educa-tion Reform Act itself since the relatively small pool of graduates in mathematics, science and technology, not to mention modern lan-guages, is increasingly attracted by better salaries and prospects to jobs outside teaching. As the senior chief inspector of Her Majesty's Inspec-torate (DES, 1989a, para 70) commented in his first annual report: 'Without [a sufficient supply of suitably qualified and competent teachers] the rest fails'. In fact, 1989 was marked in the United King-dom by a series of desperate remedies to find instant teachers for the nation's classrooms. Mature entrants or licensed teachers, without any initial teacher training, started work in September 1989 and will be followed by articled teachers or new graduates who will be similarly trained on the job but, most surprising of all, for a nation that is gener-ally reluctant to accept initiatives from the European Economic Com-munity (EEC), Britain became the first country to recognize teacher qualifications from other EEC countries and to invite the surplus teachers of Denmark, Holland and West Germany to its shores. Interestingly, tucked away in the second report on educational reform in Japan (Government of Japan, 1986, p. 21) the National Council recommends a more flexible approach to teacher supply, not to plug gaps left by an understaffed profession but to break rigidities in teacher recruitment and to bring enrichment to Japanese classrooms in the future. However, this recommendation is in line with the general tenor of the National Council's reports, which is forward-looking, innovative and idealistic, and it is to these reports that we must now finally turn.

Unlike the Education Reform Act of 1988, which is now on the statute book and is taking immediate effect in England and Wales, the Japanese reports are but recommendations of the National Council to the Government of Japan which in October 1987 published a 'Policy Outline for the Implementation of Educational Reform' and established Ministerial Conferences, project teams, consultative committees, advisory bodies and the like (Igarashi, 1988, p. 113). However, the extent to which the deliberations of these various bodies will result in radical action has yet to be seen. Meanwhile, a second way in which the reports are unlike the English Reform Act is that they do not seek to change the basic power structure of the education system as set down in previous legislation (the Fundamental Law of Education 1947), however much Prime Minister Nakasone would have liked to have returned to policies of the pre-war years, instead, they attempt to demonstrate how the Japanese, having surpassed the nations they previously sought to emulate, can confidently face the brave new world of the twenty-first century as undisputed leaders in the fields of education and economics.

The reports begin by briefly acknowledging the high international reputation gained by the success of Japan's elementary and secondary schools and by recalling the previous two periods of educational reform — in the Meiji period when the slogan was 'enrich the nation and strengthen military power' and in the post-war years when the catchphrases were 'economic rehabilitation' and 'high economic growth'. The reports then acknowledge, implicitly, that the aims of the post-war reforms have been achieved and that the educational system must now respond to the 'age of transition — transition to an internationalized society, transition to an information-centred civilization, and transition to an "80-year-career" lifestyle' (Government of Japan, 1985, p. 2). Before spelling out how this response can be made there is, by British standards, a remarkable amount of breast-beating about the 'state of confusion in education' and an open acknowledgement of most if not all of the standard criticisms about Japanese education that have been made by Western observers. For example, the first report states that 'over-emphasis on memorization in classroom instruction has prevented children from developing the ability to think and judge independently or from developing creative power. As a result, too many stereotyped people have been produced who have no distinctive personality' (Government of Japan, 1985, p. 18). The same report also cites school bullying, school violence, juvenile delinquency and school refusal as products of an excessively competitive education system, but it allows that other factors in the home and the community may play their part in social pathology. However, first and foremost the report identifies the intense competition for places at prestigious schools and universities as one of the least desirable characteristics of post-war education because it promotes a social climate where 'too much value is placed on the academic background of each person' (Government of Japan, 1985, p. 19).

That a National Council on Educational Reform should draw attention to the deleterious effects of fierce competition for elite education and that the distortion of educational opportunity should be seen as a threat to the social equilibrium of the nation rather than the hobbey-horse of a left-wing pressure group marks a third way in which the reports represent a different tradition from that of the English Reform Act. However, these contemporary Japanese sentiments are completely consistent with earlier educational reforms in the Meiji and MacArthur eras, for in 1872 the decision was made, for the good of the nation, to educate *samurai* and people together and in 1947 the Japanese accepted that compulsory comprehensive education would be the way their children were to be educated in the post-war years. Therefore the preservation of equality of opportunity in the twenty-first century in the face of the rise of the elite private schools in Japan is an important issue because hitherto it has often been assumed that economic success has been built on educational success. However, if the people of Japan lose faith in the essential fairness of public education and become aware that their nation is no longer one but two then more of the social ills of the Western nations might begin to trouble this remarkable country.

The Fourth and Final Report on Educational Reform (Government of Japan, 1987, p. 5) maintains the same lofty often spiritual tones of its predecessors as it prophesies a time in the twenty-first century when the Japanese people will prefer mental to material affluence, qualitative to quantitative affluence, and diversity and freedom of choice to uniformity and homogeneity. It goes on to predict a transition from the front-loading model of education, where education is assumed to be an activity for the early part of life only, to a life-long learning system; indeed, its recommendations cover learning from the cradle to the grave, with the promotion of education for the handicapped especially mentioned. Interestingly, many but not all of its concrete proposals for schools will have a familiar ring about them for English readers. For example, it recommends some integration of previously separate subjects in elementary schools and that courses of study for all schools be less prescriptive and allow for more creative organization and teaching. Similarly, it suggests that textbooks should allow for greater diversity in teaching and learning and should continue to be distributed freely and be subject to less screening and government control. Teacher training should be reviewed, more flexible approaches to teacher recruitment should be found, new types of secondary school such as 'all-through' schools for pupils from 12 to 18 years should be opened and universities should give more favourable consideration to graduates of vocational high schools. In all schools there should be better parent–school relationships, school facilities should be open to the community and parents should have more positive choice in the schools their children attend. Internationalization should be encouraged, English-language teaching improved and information literacy and technology should at last take their place in the nation's schools. Decentralization is positively advocated, with local government becoming more independent and innovative and local school boards becoming more vital and active. Finally, the education service is asked to come to terms with the unique Japanese experience of 'double schooling' and to consider what would be a 'desirable relationship between institutions of formal education and private education' and to decide how to deal with 'the phenomena of over-enthusiastic attendance of children at academic *juku*' (Government of Japan, 1987, p. 70). The report writers themselves clearly believe that the energy of the private sector ought to be utilized more positively while at the same time the financial burdens on parents for their children's education, often poorer parents at high school level, ought to be alleviated by tax reforms.

This final comparison of Japanese and English reforms in the 1980s has not been without surprise, since at first sight it seems that the National Council in Japan is recommending a number of practices that are commonly found in British schools, such as the integration of academic subjects, diversity of teaching methods, 'all-through' secondary schools, community colleges, parental choice and the embracing of information technology. Yet earlier in our argument we were demonstrating that several sections of the English Reform Act were advocating what in essence has been common practice in Japan for many years. However, no simple exchange of educational ideas is in prospect because the Japanese, having achieved their post-war aims of economic rehabilitation and high economic growth, are turning, in theory at least, from strategies that served the nation so well in the past to a more creative and less divisive system that will improve the quality of people's lives from the cradle to the grave. Judging by the history of this people, it would be surprising if they were not to succeed in yet another major educational reform, for we have seen how in the very beginnings of Japanese education the Chinese language and culture were successfully Japanized over the course of centuries and we have seen, too, how Western ideas were assimilated during the Meiji era and within decades made distinctively Japanese. In the case of American-style democracy and schooling it took but a few years for the Japanese to make comprehensive education their own, so who can doubt that if the will exists to act on the recommendations of the four reports on educational reform then the educational system will be transformed to produce a more creative and self-determining people? For the Japanese people long to be educated and the Japanese government knows that the health of the nation depends on this desire of the people being met.

Appendix

The open-ended questionnaire used in the comparative study described in Chapter 4 contained the following unfinished sentences spread over five sheets of A4 paper.

1 The sort of person I would most like to be like. . . . . . .
2 The sort of person I would least like to be like. . . . . . .
3 The people I am happiest with are. . . . . . .
4 The people I am unhappiest with are. . . . . . .
5 When I am by myself I. . . . . . .
6 What matters to me more than anything else. . . . . . .
7 The best thing that could happen to me. . . . . . .
8 The worst thing that could happen to me. . . . . . .
9 The best thing about life is. . . . . . .
10 The worst thing about life is. . . . . . .

In a rubric on the cover of the questionnaire the students were assured that the exercise was unrelated to school work, that their teachers would not read what they had written, that there were no right or wrong answers, that they need not give their names and that no one would criticize them for what they had written. Thus encouraged, the students wrote freely — the English more so than the Japanese, who are less used to open-ended and relatively unstructured exercises. The students' responses were analysed according to the major *themes* that emerged in each sentence and according to the *values* that were expressed in the themes. In an open-ended questionnaire of this sort where the respondents are free to develop their own ideas a *theme* is considered a major one if it appears in 10 per cent or more of the papers from one of the two countries being compared. *Values*, on the other hand, are assessed differently and are discussed at the end of Chapter 4 and below. A summary analysis of *themes* appears in Table 1 and of *values* in Table 2.

Table 1 Dominant themes, both shared and unshared, by country and by sentence, from the comparative study

Sentences	Shared and unshared themes	English study			Japanese Study			Level of significance
		Males (N = 492)	Females (N = 328)	Total (%)	Males (N = 150)	Females (N = 133)	Total (%)	
1	'Myself' choices	80	75	155 19	1	—	1 0.3	**
2	Politicians	48	37	85 10	3	—	3 1	**
3	Friends	224	205	429 52	72	62	134 47	NS
	Family	153	170	323 39	20	24	44 16	**
4	Teachers	38	23	61 7	12	4	16 6	NS
	Family	14	34	48 6	4	4	8 3	NS
5	Listen to music	165	135	300 37	37	60	97 34	NS
	Read	131	121	252 31	45	63	108 38	NS
	Watch TV	142	85	227 28	69	52	121 43	**
	Sleep				35	18	53 19	
	Studying				14	11	25 9	
6	Family	143	119	262 32	6	7	13 5	**
	Friends	87	95	182 22	16	32	48 17	NS
	Getting a job	53	65	118 14	8	1	9 3	**
	Studying				29	31	60 21	
	Entering high school				25	18	43 15	
	Exams				8	6	14 5	

Table 1 continued

Sentences	Shared and unshared themes	English study				Japanese Study				Level of significance
		Males (N = 492)	Females (N = 328)	Total	(%)	Males (N = 150)	Females (N = 133)	Total	(%)	
7	Getting a job	128	97	225	27	4	2	6	2	**
	Entering high school					28	35	63	22	*
	Money	103	42	145	18	22	7	29	10	
	Passing exams	86	60	146	18					
8	Death of relatives	95	90	185	23	7	14	21	7	**
	Personal disablement	93	71	164	20	11	6	17	6	**
	Own death	84	45	129	16	39	18	57	20	NS
	Unemployment	62	45	107	13	3	1	4	1	**
	Failing exams	49	53	102	13	33	39	72	25	**
9	Enjoyment	75	62	137	17	4	10	14	5	**
	Friends	51	73	124	15	39	39	78	28	**
	Living	50	42	92	11	20	27	47	17	**
	Marriage	12	7	19	2					
10	Death	99	74	173	21	76	45	121	43	**
	School	62	48	110	13					
	War	30	60	90	11	10	12	22	8	NS
	Violence	30	51	81	10					

* $df = 1, p < 0.01$ ** $df = 1, p < 0.001$

Table 2 Summary of Chi-Square Analyses of Values

Differences between groups in response to sentences 1–4 and 6–10	Levels of significance				
	$p > 0.05$	$p < 0.05$	$p < 0.02$	$p < 0.01$	$p < 0.001$
English males and females		4	2		1,3,6,7,8,9,10
Japanese males and females	3	1,4,6,8	2	7,9	10
English and Japanese males	10		7	9	1,2,3,4,6,8
English and Japanese females	3,6,9	4	7,8		1,2,10
English and Japanese males and females				9	1,2,3,4, 6,7,8,10

Numbers in the table refer to individual sentence numbers of the questionnaire. The differences between sentences listed in the right-hand columns are, statistically, the most significant while those in the left-hand column are the least so.

In the English study there were striking differences between the values expressed by the two sexes. These differences were always significant, not in the sense that they were necessarily important, but in the statistical sense that they were unlikely, to a known extent, to have arisen by chance. The statistical test of significance chosen for the present study, the chi-square test, is widely used for data like mine because it can test the difference between the actual scores and what might have been expected had all things been equal. In Tables 1 and 2 the differences are expressed in terms of scores which range from those that are not significant (NS), through to those which are highly significant ($p < 0.001$). Thus Table 2 reveals that there was a significant difference between the values expressed by the English males and females in response to all sentences but that in sentences 1, 3, 6, 7, 8, 9, 10 we know that less than once in a thousand times could these have arisen by chance.

In the Japanese study similar differences were found but not to the same degree for it was only in sentence 10 that differences were significant at the 0.001 level. Here it was caused by Japanese boys interpreting the worst things about life more in terms of personal injury and misfortune than the Japanese girls, who were apt to think in terms of damage to interpersonal relationships and of calamities to others. But in sentences 1, 4, 6 and 8 of the Japanese survey the difference between the sexes was not so great and could have arisen by chance less than once in 20 times. It would seem, therefore, that Japanese males and females are generally closer in their valuing than their English counterparts while at the same time being significantly different from the English, except that the males in the two surveys differ from each other more than the females. However, the direction of these differences varies. In sentence 1, for example, as in sentence 3, the difference was caused by more Japanese students choosing values such as *kindness* instead of the more common English choice of *popularity*. Again in sentences 2 and 4 the Japanese were more likely to choose least ideals such as *selfishness* than the peculiarly English values of *snobbishness* and *bigheadedness*. But in sentence 6 a change of direction occurred because of heavy Japanese nominations for *entering high school* compared with the valuation placed by the English on their love for their *parents*. This change of direction was repeated in sentence 8, where the English again emphasized their regard for their *parents*, but not in sentence 7 where nearly a quarter of the English — compared with about a tenth of the Japanese — expressed materialistic values. Finally, in sentences 9 and 10 a last reversal took place because the English expressed fewer material and personal values than the Japanese and more interpersonal, social and humanitarian concerns.

References

Azuma, H. (1986) 'Why Study Child Development in Japan?' in Stevenson *et al.* (1986).

BBC TV (1989) *'Hirohito: Behind the Myth'*, 24 January. BBC1.

Beauchamp, E.R. (1987) 'The Development of Japanese Educational Policy 1945–85', *History of Education Quarterly*, 27, 3, 299–324.

Befu, H. (1986) 'The Social and Cultural Background of Child Development in Japan and the United States' in Stevenson *et al.* (1986).

Bird, I. (1984) *Unbeaten Tracks in Japan*. Virago, London (First published by John Murray, 1880).

Cantor, L. (1989) *Vocational Education and Training in the Developed World. A Comparative Study*. Routledge, London.

CBI (1989) *Towards a Skills Revolution: A Youth Charter*. CBI, London.

City and Guilds of London Institute (1987). *Employers' Guide to a New Qualification*. CPVE City and Guilds, London.

Comber, L.C. and Keeves, J. (1973) *Science Achievement in Nineteen Countries*. John Wiley, New York.

Cox, S. (1983) 'Japan's infernal exam system', *New Society*, 64, 1076, 508.

DES (1972) *Education: A Framework for Expansion*, Cmnd 5174. HMSO, London.

DES (1975) *A Language for Life*. HMSO, London.

DES (1988a) *Mathematics for Ages 5 to 16*. HMSO, London.

DES (1988b) *Statistical Bulletin*, 14/88, December. London.

DES (1989a) *Standards in Education 1987–1988*. London.

DES (1989b) *National Curriculum: From Policy to Practice*. London.

DES (1989c) *Discipline in Schools: Report of the Committee of Enquiry Chaired by Lord Elton*. HMSO, London.

Dore, R.P. (1965) *Education in Tokugawa Japan*. Routledge & Kegan Paul, London.

Duke, B. (1986) *The Japanese School: Lessons for Industrial America*. New York, Praeger.

Edwards, J.B. (1973) 'Chosen ideal person, least ideal person, and judgements about moral wickedness: a developmental study', *Journal of Moral Education*, 3, 1, 379–99.

Ejima, M. (1988) 'Problems of Educating for a Caring Community in Contemporary Japan', *New Era in Education*, 69, 2, 55–7.

Gordon, B. (1987) 'Cultural Comparisons of Schooling', *Educational Researcher*, 16, 6, 4–7.

Government of Japan (1985) *First Report on Educational Reform*. Tokyo.

Government of Japan (1986) *Second Report on Educational Reform*. Tokyo.

Government of Japan (1987) *Fourth and Final Report on Educational Reform of the National Council on Educational Reform*. Tokyo.

Hargreaves, D.H. (1981) 'Unemployment, Leisure and Education', *Oxford Review of Education*, 7, 3, 197–208.

Hardwick, M. (1970) *Discovery of Japan*. Hamlyn, London.

Havighurst, R.J. and Taba, H. (1949) *Adolescence Character and Personality*. Wiley, New York.

Hayes, C. *et al.* (1984) *Competence and Competition: Training and Education in the Federal Republic of Germany, the United States and Japan*. National Economic Development Council, London.

Hendry, J. (1986) *Becoming Japanese*. Manchester University Press, Manchester.

Hewitt, B. & Takayama, H. (1988) 'Testing the Rules in Japan', *Newsweek*, 30 May, 26.

Hirose, T. and Hatta, T. (1988) 'Reading Disabilities in Modern Japanese Children', *Journal of Research in Reading*, 11, 2, 152–60.

House of Commons Education, Science and Arts Committee (1988) *Educational Provision for the Under Fives*, HC 30, Sess. 1988–9. HMSO, London.

Igarashi, K. (1988) 'Recent Trends in Educational Reform', *International Journal of Educational Research*, 12, 2, 109–14.

Ikuo, A. (1986) 'The Dilemma of Japanese Education Today', *The Japan Foundation Newsletter*, 13, 5, 1–10.

Ishiguro, K. (1986) *An Artist of the Floating World*. Faber and Faber, London.

Kaigo, T. (1968) *Japanese Education: Its Past and Present*. Kokusai Banka Shinkokai, Tokyo.

Kashiwagi, K. (1986) 'Personality Development of Adolescents' in Stevenson *et al.* (1986).

Kobayashi, T. (1976) *Society, Schools and Progress in Japan*. Pergamon, Oxford.

Kojima, H. (1986) 'Child Rearing Concepts as a Belief-Value System of the Society and the Individual' in Stevenson *et al.* (1986).

Lambert, C. (1989) '*The Japanese Education System*' Unpublished final-year Education and Mathematics project, Loughborough University.

Leestma, R. *et al.* (1987) *Japanese Education Today*. US Department of Education, Washington, DC.

Lewis, C.C. (1988) 'Japanese First-Grade Classrooms: Implications for US

Theory and Research', *Comparative Education Review*, 32, 2, 159–72.

Lowndes, G.A.N. (1969) *The Silent Society Revolution*. Oxford University Press, Oxford.

Lynn, R. (1988) *Educational Achievement in Japan: Lessons for the West*. London, Macmillan.

Maclure, S. (1988) *Education Re-formed*, Hodder and Stoughton, London.

Manthorpe, V. (ed) (1986) *The Japanese Diaries of Richard Gordon Smith* Viking/Rainbow, Harmondsworth, Middlesex.

McCormick, K. (1988) 'Vocationalism and the Japanese Educational System', *Comparative Education*, 24, 1, 37–51.

Morrell, F. (1989) *Children of the future*. Hogarth Press, London.

Narumiya, C. (1986) 'Opportunites for Girls and Women in Japanese Education', *Comparative Education*, 22, 1, 47–52.

NIER (1988) *Basic Facts and Figures about the Educational System in Japan*. National Institute for Educational Research, Tokyo.

Nishi, T. (1982) *Unconditional Democracy — Education and Politics in Occupied Japan, 1945-1952*. Hoover Institution Press, Stanford University, California.

Nishimura, H. (1985) 'Commissioning a Master Plan', *Japan Quarterly*, 32, 1, 18–22.

OECD (1971) *Reviews of National Policies for Education. Japan*. Paris.

Okuda, S. and Hishimura, Y. (1983) 'The Development of Secondary Education in Japan after World War II', *Higher Education*, 12, 567–78.

Passin, H. (1965) *Society and Education in Japan*. Teachers College Press, Columbia University/US Government Printing Office, Washington, DC.

Prais, S.J. (1986) 'Education for Productivity: Comparisons of Japanese and English Schooling and Vocational Preparation', *Compare*, 16, 2, 121–47.

Reeves, M.S. (ed.) (1985) 'Schooling in Japan: The Paradox in the Pattern', *Education Week*, 27 February, 11–26.

Rohlen, T.P. (1983) *Japan's High Schools*. University of California Press, Berkeley.

Rutter, M. (1979) *Changing Youth in a Changing Society*. Nuffield Provincial Hospitals Trust, London.

Shimahara N.K. (1979) *Adaptation and Education in Japan*. Praeger, New York.

Shimahara, N. (1984) 'Toward the Equality of a Japanese Minority: the Case of the Burakumin', *Comparative Education*, 20, 3, 339–53.

Simmons, C. and Wade, W. (1984) *I Like to Say what I Think: A Study of the Attitudes, Values and Beliefs of Young People Today*. Kogan Page, London.

Simmons, C. and Wade, W. (1988) 'Contrasting Attitudes to Education in England and Japan', *Educational Research*, 30, 2, 146–52.

Singleton, J. (1967) *Nichu: A Japanese School*. Holt, Rinehart and Winston, New York.

Smith R.J. (1983) *Japanese Society*. Cambridge University Press, Cambridge.

Stevenson, H. *et al.* (eds) (1986) *Child Development and Education in Japan*. W.H. Freeman, New York.

Stigler, J. *et al.* (1982) 'Curriculum and Achievement in Mathematics: A Study of Elementary School Children in Japan, Taiwan and the United States', *Journal of Educational Psychology*, 74, 315–22.

Storry, R.(1976) *A History of Modern Japan*. Penguin, Harmondsworth.

Thatcher, M. (1987) 'AIDS education and the year 2000!', *Women's Own*, 31 October, 8–10.

Tsukada, M. (1988) 'Institutionalised Supplementary Education in Japan: the *Yobiko* and *Ronin* Student Adaptations', *Comparative Education*, 24, 3, 285–303.

Wardle, D. (1970) *English Popular Education 1780–1970*. Cambridge University Press, Cambridge.

White, M. (1987) *The Japanese Educational Challenge: A Commitment to Children*. The Free Press, A Division of Macmillan Inc., New York.

White, M. and LeVine, R. (1986) 'What is an *Ii Ko* (Good Child)?' in Stevenson *et al.* (1986).

Yamamura, Y. (1986) 'The Child in Japanese Society' in Stevenson *et al.* (1986).

Yuuki, M. (1987) 'Out-of-School Supplementary Education in Japan', *Research Bulletin of the National Institute for Educational Research, Tokyo*, 25, 21–31.

Index